R

19

15

SOUTH DEVON

Combe, Tor and Seascape

By the same author:

SOUTH DEVON

Combe, Tor and Seascape

by

ANNE BORN

LONDON
VICTOR GOLLANCZ LTD
1983

British Library Cataloguing in Publication Data
Born, Anne
   South Devon.
   1. Devon—Description and travel
   I. Title
   914.23'5   DA670.D5
   ISBN 0-575-03249-9

MAPS

Christopher Saxton, who was born in 1542, was the first cartographer to make printed maps of the counties of England. He was authorized to do the work by Queen Elizabeth I, and his maps are remarkably accurate for their time, as well as being decoratively delightful.

I am grateful to the Bodleian Library, Oxford, for permission to reproduce Saxton's map of Devon.

Andrew Maden has drawn the modern map and I wish to record my thanks for the care he has given to the task.

The poems "Michelcombe Lane to the Moor" and "Cave" are reprinted by permission of the Editors of *Envoi* and *Other Poetry*.

Printed in Great Britain at
The Camelot Press Ltd, Southampton

for Pat

SOUTH DEVON

Combe, Tor and Seascape

By the same author:

... this place that doth inspire

Michael Drayton
Polyolbion, on Devonshire

Contents

Illustrations

Unless otherwise indicated, illustrations are reproduced by permission of the British Tourist Authority.

PRESCRIPT

I WAS INTRODUCED to Devon when I was ten. That was the start of one of those relationships that grow stronger and more obsessive with each year that passes; and the trouble with Devon is that its complex beauty makes it hard to deal with rationally. Everything is richer and more highly-charged here: geology, climate, scenery, vegetation, archaeology, history, people. . . .

But I try in this book to describe some of the characteristics of this place that are particularly absorbing to me. When I was considering the shape of the subject-matter, I glanced at a picture my daughter Carrie had made for me a year or two earlier. It was a composite of pieces of photography forming a theme: the textures of houses, and water. There are sections of roofs, of walls, and of river and sea. I realized then what she had been at: perceptively making a portrait of my preferred settings, and thus in a sense of me.

As well as with the region, its towns and landscapes, I am concerned to consider the lives of Devonshire people from earliest times through their houses, in the various forms and styles to be found in South Devon, from Bronze Age hut to a 1980s' theatre; and to explore the waterways, whether sea, rivers, streams or lakes.

Many kind friends have accompanied me, both old and new. I am grateful to all; most especially to the *genius loci* of Devonshire.

Oxford/Salcombe 1982

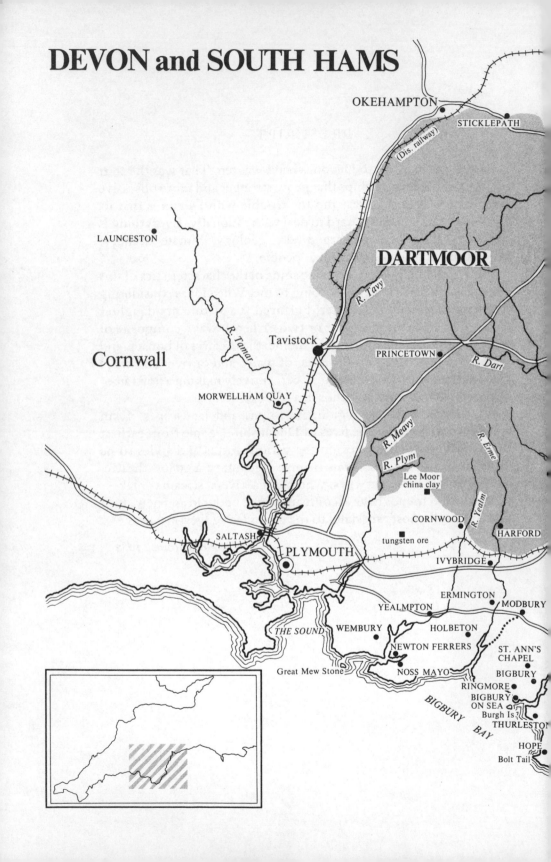

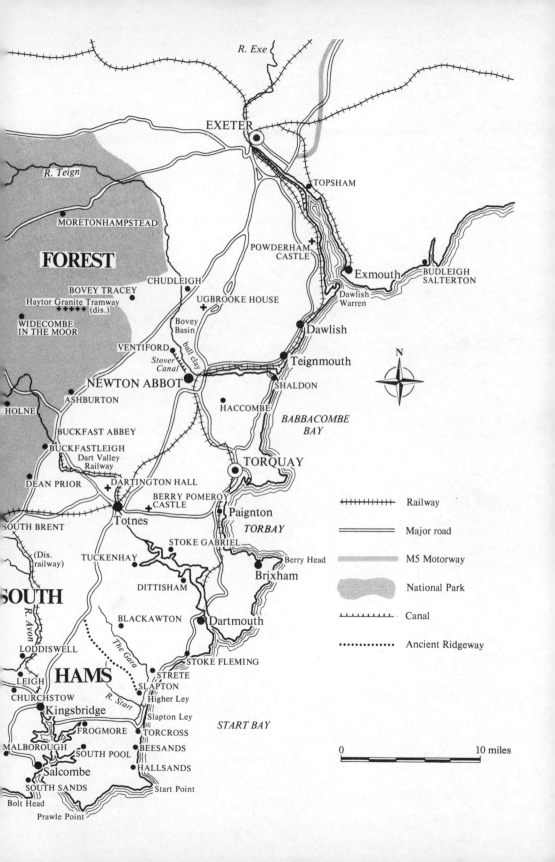

R. Exe

EXETER

TOPSHAM

R. Teign

MORETONHAMPSTEAD

FOREST

POWDERHAM
CASTLE

Exmouth

BUDLEIGH
SALTERTON

CHUDLEIGH

BOVEY TRACEY

Haytor Granite Tramway
(dis.)

UGBROOKE HOUSE

Dawlish
Warren

WIDECOMBE
IN THE MOOR

*Bovey
Basin*

Dawlish

VENTIFORD

ball clay

*Stover
Canal*

Teignmouth

NEWTON ABBOT

SHALDON

ASHBURTON

HACCOMBE

HOLNE

*BABBACOMBE
BAY*

BUCKFAST ABBEY

BUCKFASTLEIGH

Dart Valley
Railway

TORQUAY

DEAN PRIOR

DARTINGTON HALL

BERRY POMEROY
CASTLE

Paignton

SOUTH BRENT

Totnes

TORBAY

(Dis.
railway)

STOKE GABRIEL

Berry Head

TUCKENHAY

Brixham

R. Avon

DITTISHAM

SOUTH

BLACKAWTON

Dartmouth

LODDISWELL

The Gara

STOKE FLEMING

LEIGH

HAMS

STRETE

CHURCHSTOW

R. Start

SLAPTON

Higher Ley

Kingsbridge

Slapton Ley

FROGMORE

TORCROSS

START BAY

MALBOROUGH

SOUTH POOL

BEESANDS

Salcombe

HALLSANDS

SOUTH SANDS

Start Point

Bolt Head

Prawle Point

N

Railway

Major road

M5 Motorway

National Park

Canal

Ancient Ridgeway

0   10 miles

CONTRARY WINDS

The headland is a triangle's apex,
its sides defined by ria, moor and sea.
Here eyes are winged, widened
to see as angel, astronaut or fly.

Clouds inhabit this sky hugely.
From south out of the blue, cumulus
expands from some celestial whisk,
slowly breasts space with whiteness.

But from north and in a lower sphere
black rags of angstclouds rushing below
the white, blown by the last gasp
of winter, going fast and low

in the other direction, cast their shadow
over lamb, primrose, lark and grass.
Memento mori as counterbalance
to spring words and flowering face.

Chapter One

THE LAND AND WEATHER MAP

IF THE MAP is tilted to the left South Devon assumes roughly the shape of Britain, with Exeter at John o' Groats and Plymouth at Land's End. The eastern limit is the English Channel, the western the A38 road that skirts the southern border of Dartmoor National Park.

Geographically Exeter represents a kind of watershed. It is bounded on the east and south by the ring road extension of the M5 that now brings great tides of traffic surging from the east and north to the West Country and that cuts through the red sandstone that never fails to warm the returning heart. Then the climb up the steep chert and flint ridge of Haldon opens out a wide view of Dartmoor and the lowlands to the south. The flat Taunton plain has given way to hills, moors and valleys, the colours of grass and soil brighten, air and water are softer. It is hard for the non-geologist to visualize this apparently ageless landscape in the processes of gigantic upheaval and mutation that went to its making and millions of years ago laid the foundations of what we see today. But even a cursory study of the earth's surface formation adds enormously to the appreciation not only of topography but of all the facets of our life: history, architecture, agriculture, as well as scenery.

Devon is a terraced landscape. The top layer is the central, massive granite batholith of Dartmoor with its great rounded heights, wooded valleys and cleaves, tors and blanket bogs. Its average height is 1300 feet. The peat bogs that formed on the hills yielded only poor agricultural land; the valleys that cut deeply into them were steep enough to provide good shelter for trees but impossible conditions for cultivation.

But the drowned valleys or rias of the estuaries reach far inland bringing mild conditions from the sea. Furthest south, the low-lying South Hams forming the southernmost tip of the Devonshire coastline receive especially mild conditions induced by their sheltered position, the surrounding North Atlantic Drift and the prevailing mild south-westerly winds.

The geology of this southernmost part of Devon is divided rather satisfyingly in the form of a sandwich. It is thus fairly uniformly structured, although various tongues and intrusions of different rocks break up the basic pattern here and there. The largest sections are formed of sandstones and limestones of the Devonian period, and these, with the granite of Dartmoor, are very ancient rocks of up to 400 million years old. In the east of the region, and particularly in the area in and around the Bovey Basin, newer rock types, including the red land produced by the new red sandstones, marls and breccias, are interspersed with the old in smaller areas, creating a kaleidoscope of varying colours on the extremely complicated geological map of Devon.

Granite is an igneous rock formed in plutonic conditions under great heat; it is made up of three components: translucent grey quartz crystals, white feldspar and mica, the glittering particles. It contains none of the fossil remains of life forms that were once vital for determining age and conditions at various periods. The bedded rocks, sandstone, limestone and grits, are the ones that have preserved the fossils.

There are five extrusions of granite in the South-West Peninsula: Dartmoor in Devon, Bodmin, Hensbarrow, Carnmenellis and Penwith, at Land's End, in Cornwall. (Exmoor is sandstone.) These form a curved backbone to the peninsula and the granite uplands are like great vertebrae protruding from the land's back.

Along a line running fairly straight west to east from Plymouth to Torbay the Middle Devonian rocks give way to a layer of Meadfoot Beds of slates and sandstone; below these is a layer of Dartmouth slate and shale beds tapering off towards the west, followed by another of Meadfoot. Finally, the southernmost section of the sandwich is a layer stretching about three miles from south to north of a completely different kind of rock, metamorphic schists, from Bolt Tail to Torcross. This is unlike granite and is formed in conditions of great pressure, as deep as ten miles below the earth's surface. It contains mica and veins and clots of quartz, but is grouped in flaky layers, so that the soil around Salcombe, for instance, although quite productive, is full of shard-like fragments, draining like a sponge with gargantuan sucking powers. The schists form the incomparably grand scenery of this stretch of the coast, centrally divided and penetrated by

Salcombe estuary whose longest branch extends as far inland as Kingsbridge.

The reaction between erosion and the alignment of the schists after their final upheaval has left them here with their sharp extremities pointing east; in places the cliff walls appear to have been cut off with a saw, so straight is the still jagged surface. But the tops of the Bolt Head cliffs form almost horizontal points and pinnacles, many of which have the shape of petrified eagle heads eternally watching the sunrise. Off the northern end of Starehole Bay a large rock is topped by another smaller round one, "Queen Victoria's Head", covered with golden lichen hair and looking approvingly over the Bar, believed to have been celebrated by her favourite Tennyson in his poem "Crossing the Bar".

On Bolt Head, on the west side of the estuary mouth, there is a granite memorial to a local resident, Walter Newton Drew, with a bronze dial inscribed with the points of the compass and the distances to a number of places, including Hay Tor, twenty-five miles away, Exeter Cathedral, Ushant and Guernsey. If you stand here facing north you have an inspiring view inland. On the skyline is Dartmoor, more often than not topped by a dramatic cloudbank; if there is sunshine, the china clay waste heaps glitter on its western limit, and if it's a clear day you can pick out Hay Tor and other summits. Below the moor the land descends in stages like platforms and spreads towards the sea in a great patchwork that is a delight to the eye. It is good at all times of the year, although in late summer the contrasting colours of ripe grain, pasture and dark woods are most striking. It is never the same, and each time you take the cliff walk from Salcombe, along the lower Courtenay Walk halfway up the 400-foot high cliffs to Starehole Bay, up its valley and back along the top of the cliffs past the memorial (or you can reverse the route; whichever way we take, we call it The Round) the pleasure will be unique. On one day that I recall particularly clearly there were winds at varying heights driving two different types of cloud layers in opposite directions at speed in a stormy aerial confusion.

Two miles to the west rises the spire of Malborough Church, a landmark that dominates the landscape for many miles and that suddenly confronts the traveller from innumerable angles and viewpoints from the maze of surrounding lanes for up to twenty miles' distance. Below, the estuary drives inland, its relative calm welcoming sailors who come into the harbour in a ceaseless procession throughout spring, summer and autumn. In bad weather the bar inside the estuary mouth breaks roaring across its width in ferocious combers.

Kingsbridge is just out of sight here, snugly sited at the head of the furthest inland point reached by one of the eight creek-heads. There is no river, and this "estuary" is in fact a ria, or drowned valley. But streams run down to all the creek-heads through deep combes, a number of them still moderately well wooded. It is the combes (OE *cumb*, a hollow) that gives South Devon its particular personality and, to an extent, its private mystery despite thousands of years of human interference. This quality of secrecy, that has attracted me to the place all my life, can still frequently consent to drop its guard and reveal some new discovery – a seacave, a different amazing view, another beautiful house in a remote setting in a state varying from total ruin to loving restoration.

The Bolt Head panorama with its prevalent cumulus mass in the north is a demonstration of the most usual weather conditions – not that South Devon weather is any more easily predictable or less changeable than that of the rest of Britain. But it is a fact that it is milder than anywhere else, with Salcombe the warmest place of all owing to its southernmost protected site and its estuary. The annual mean temperature is about 11° C on the coast and 10° C inland, and winter temperatures are a degree or so higher than those "upcountry". Frost is less frequent and snow even less so except on Dartmoor, where of course very harsh conditions obtain in winter, and where farmers are constantly losing valuable sheep stock. But there have been a few winters marked by terrible blizzards even in the south: 1881, 1891, 1927, 1929, 1947 and 1978. In 1978 even at Salcombe the snow filled lanes up to a height of six feet, and roads were impassable for several days; thousands of gallons of milk had to be thrown away and thousands of birds, including flocks of redstarts caught by the storm, died. Most dramatic of all, the ammil covered every smallest twig and pine cone. Ammil is a dialect word possibly derived from enamel, which is certainly its effect; Dartmoor foresters are familiar with it in most winters, but in the south it is extremely rare. In 1978 our blue pine turned into an orchestra as the pendant ice drops and icicles tolled and chinked against each other, and all the trees shone like prisms. Then the following winter unusually fierce gales destroyed many fine trees.

Two years earlier, South Devon, with the rest of Europe, suffered from the Great Drought when water supplies practically dried up and many trees, shrubs and plants were lost. The earth cracked open dramatically in the fields, houses developed cracks as foundations shrank, and wild life suffered as well as farm stock. I saw the unusual sight of a raven circling above a Salcombe valley being mobbed by half a dozen kestrels. Ravens are quite a rare sight nowadays in the South Hams and I imagine this one had flown down from the moor in search of carrion.

Whether or not weather conditions are changing dramatically, it must be admitted that there are many soft, grey, damp days throughout the year and plentiful rainfall, more of it on the moor than at lower levels. When it rains in South Devon it makes "a proper job" of it. Yet because of the scenery, the lushness of the vegetation, the comparative mildness and the wonderful aromatic air, it is never as grim as in other regions. Fog, when it occurs, is dangerous on the moors and the sea. Sea mist can sweep in suddenly and stealthily and cover a sunlit scene with its clammy blindfold in the middle of a brilliant day. It's a curious experience to be becalmed in thick fog off Plymouth with a submarine throbbing by on one side of the boat and invisible voices apparently a couple of yards away on a beach the other side!

South-westerly winds are the norm and can mould ridge and hilltop trees by their constant smoothing. But there is a fair amount of easterly and northerly wind as well, bringing crisp air and often longer periods of cloudless weather.

Chapter Two

EXETER – COUNTY GATEWAY

THE ROMANS HALTED their westward march through Britain to found the city of Isca about AD 50, and did not push much further west in their colonizing activities. After they left, the town became the Isca Dumnoniorum of the Celtic Dumnonii. The Romans built on the site of an earlier settlement, as the hilltop position overlooking a river, and various finds, indicate. A lull followed their departure and then the town grew steadily. Through most of the medieval period it remained within the confines of the Roman walls, three-quarters of which, although much overworked by repairs, still stand today.

Geologically the country immediately around Exeter is a blend of outcrops of New Red Sandstone and ridges of shales and grits, with a few small patches of basaltic volcanic material, known locally as "trap rock", to the north and west. A number of the remaining older buildings, the charming small city churches, and the gate-house that stands as a reminder of the Norman Rougemont Castle, are a mellow rose-crimson.

Like Plymouth, Exeter has seen violence, during the Civil War, and in World War Two, when it was savagely bombed on the night of 5 May 1942, mostly with incendiary bombs. A great part of the city centre was burned. Fortunately there was not a very high death toll, although eighty people lost their lives. It was a repeat in some ways of the burning of the infant town by the Danes in 1003; and the Cathedral was badly damaged, a bomb exploded in the Chapel of St James on the south side. Perhaps it was miraculous that it was no worse, and the damage was all repaired.

The Cathedral Close was relatively unharmed, as were a good many of the unique buildings from the medieval period onwards in nearby High Street. Some of the beautiful eighteenth-century streets were wiped out, but on the whole Exeter suffered much less than Plymouth, and the heart of the city survived. The buildings of the Close, all in use and good health, form a chronology of English architecture from medieval to modern, each building asserting a definite, almost always pleasing, character. Despite this variety the Close exhibits a homogeneity that nicely illustrates the happy-go-lucky English genius of design; and its presence protects the west and north sides of the Cathedral from being dwarfed and seriously overshadowed by modern development. The main ring road runs well to the west.

The material chiefly used in the building of the Cathedral, including the magnificent west front, was Beer freestone. This is a granular limestone from the ancient quarries in the chalk at Beer in East Devon, a beautiful creamy stone that grows whiter with exposure. The two great Norman towers consecrated in 1133 were retained in the chief rebuilding operations carried out from about 1270 to 1360. From then on the Cathedral has stood as the centre of Christianity in Devon, a spiritual and artistic power house that never fails to impress.

The first bishop of Exeter was Leofric, installed in 1050 by Edward the Confessor; he was a devoted bishop and cultivated man who bequeathed to the Cathedral library its most precious possession, the Exeter Book. This superbly illuminated manuscript book, still kept in the Cathedral library now situated in part of the red sandstone Bishop's palace on the south side of the Cathedral, contains the largest collection of Anglo-Saxon poems known to exist. The library also holds the Exeter Domesday Book, of about 1086.

The early bishops who followed Leofric, remembered as much for their work as by their tombs in the Cathedral, included Bronescombe, Stapeldon, Grandisson. They were responsible for the development of the Cathedral in the thirteenth and fourteenth centuries. They also energetically supervised the churches in their see and, during this period of consolidation of market towns and growth of commerce, granted many charters and permissions to hold fairs. From the thirteenth to the sixteenth century the majority of Devonshire parish churches were being built or rebuilt with native stone: Beerstone in the east and as decoration and interior work where it could be transported along the coast by sea, sandstone in the Exeter area and down towards Paignton where the red vein reaches the sea, limestone in the Torquay and Plymouth areas, and slate and schists in the south. Their towers and spires have been landmarks and focal points for five or six hundred years; no wonder they are such an integral part of the landscape, seeming in their natural local settings as permanent as the cliffs and tors.

The long line of succeeding bishops grew, in each century there were new decorations, tombs, arrangements in the Cathedral, additions and embellishments to the interior – the glory of the immensely long vaulted nave ceiling, the elaborate yet not over-elaborate arcades, the east window, the minstrels' gallery, the stained glass, the stone and wood sculpture.

The immense fourteenth-century wooden bishop's throne, a small cathedral in itself, in which the wood is treated more as stone in the construction method, would have been painted in bright medieval colours and had a less ponderous effect than the darkened wood gives now; the misericord seats of the choir stalls are astounding in the inventiveness of their carved ornamentation. Many of the themes derive from secular life here as elsewhere, but there are some with mythological figures, and a few of these, where grotesque masks branch into dual bodies with webbed feet, or birds with hand-like claws, or sprays of foliage, are directly reminiscent of Hieronymus Bosch in their surrealism and menace. On one, the Exeter elephant may be the first artistic representation of that animal in England.

The fifteenth-century clock in the north transept represents the sun and moon in pre-Copernican orbit around the earth, telling the hour and the phase of the moon. Its motto, "pereunt et imputantur", means "the hours perish and are reckoned to our account".

On the exterior of the Cathedral, the west window and below it the double tier of niched figures form Exeter's particular feature. The west front is so wide that, with the spaced twin Norman towers, it has an immensely solid air – where Salisbury is soaring, Exeter is massive – and *yet*, the delicate pinnacles of the towers and the graceful flying buttresses of the clerestory give it movement, preclude heaviness.

The Cathedral is a relatively new building in this part of the city. The Roman military bath house was situated under the grass of the present spacious Close; it was a sophisticated building, a sports complex in fact, with facilities for various forms of exercise as well as the baths and heated rooms. It was excavated in 1971–73, but it was not found possible to leave it uncovered, and so the remains, chiefly consisting of the complex heating system, were protected with sand and covered over again.

Six of Exeter's once numerous little medieval city churches remain, all fairly close and to the north and west of the Cathedral. Its gleaming maternal grandeur dwarfs them, but I find them quite as beautiful in their serviceable native New Red Sandstone breccia, roughly dressed in soft crimson. Much of their stone was quarried at nearby Heavitree; but although their walls are built of the same material, each has its distinctive architectural style and personality. The foundation of these churches may go back to pre-Saxon times, although most of their present form is fifteenth-century.

St Martin's is in the north corner of the Cathedral close, near the SPCK bookshop and the Ship Inn that, according to tradition, was frequented by Sir Francis Drake when he was in Exeter, and next to the Elizabethan house called Mol's Coffee House, from 1596. The church is set obliquely to the street and buildings round it, which at once gives it character; it has a fifteenth-century barrel-vaulted roof with good carved bosses; but most of the furnishings are seventeenth- and eighteenth-century, and include a gallery, box-pews and pulpit, and some quite impressive monuments. These impose a strongly civic air on this little church, situated as it still is in the centre of the busy commercial life of the city.

St Petrock's, on the east side of the Close, and whose saint has several other dedications in Devon including the church adjoining Dartmouth Castle, is an even more asymmetric shape, less attractive than St Martin's. A short distance from here down Fore Street is St Olave's, named for St Olaf, a christianized Viking king and later patron saint of Norway. It may have been a house-chapel for King Canute's sister-in-law Gytha, Countess of Wessex. The little square tower, oddly positioned in the sanctuary, may date from the original eleventh-century building. St Olave's' romantic charm seems suited to its present-day high church habit, in contrast to broad civic St Martin's.

A little way back off Fore Street to the left is St Mary Arches, probably so called from the beautiful twelfth-century Romanesque double-chamfered arches on each side of the nave, the earliest of their kind in Devon. Their stone is paler pink than the exteriors, and the church, although much altered in the course of the centuries, is light and airy. In common with St Martin's it has a low church civic tradition, and contains among its interesting memorials an effigy of sixteenth-century Thomas Andrew, twice mayor of Exeter, master of the guild of Merchant Venturers. Another effigy is of Thomas Walker, three times mayor, who died in 1628, and his wife, with a memorial poem that plays on their name:

> Affecte they that can challenge none
> Gvilded titles on a stone
> Mortals keep yovr annals jvste
> This paire shall ever scorne times rvste
> In them after ages may
> Reade what this stone sparth to say
> Here ly two walkers now at reste
> By whose covrse of life expressed
> A straiter way to blisse then all
> Those that yov walking sages call
> Byth steps of these farre readyer yov may
> Then thothers rules finde heavens milky way.

The responsible civic tradition of St Mary Arches continues today in its function as the book repository and office of the diocesan education centre.

The new redbrick Guildhall shopping precinct covers a considerable area between North Street, High Street and Queen Street, its main entrance formed by the enormous cream-painted classical façade with Doric columns of the Victorian Higher Market, in Queen Street. In the paved central open space, surrounded by all the usual giant stores and multi-storey carpark, is a toytown church, diminutive St Pancras, which consists merely of nave and chancel, built of very rough blocks of Heavitree stone, probably from the twelfth century although its dedication indicates a previous much earlier church. The inscription on the bell in the small bell-tower at the west end proclaims stoutly: "Although I am small, I am heard over a great distance", and it stands as an instance of survival and strength, a haven of peace and faith, in which services are held and people may find quietness in the heat of the day.

The sixth central city church, St Stephen's in the High Street's east end, has an eleventh-century crypt, now closed, but the church was completely rebuilt in 1664 after a fire, and practically rebuilt again after World War Two, apart from some interior furnishings. It is used for a variety of purposes as well as services.

In addition to the Cathedral Close, Fore Street, that becomes High Street at the central crossroads where North and South Streets meet, is a unique collection of living architecture. On the south side, Tudor merchants' houses are disguised at ground-floor level with modern windows, but projecting upper storeys reveal their age. The Guildhall in the High Street, roughly parallel with the Close, is one of the finest buildings, and one of the oldest municipal houses, in Britain, although the fourteenth- and fifteenth-century hall is concealed behind an ornately decorated Elizabethan porch, its first-floor pillared front with mullion windows supported on an arcade extending over the pavement. Despite Victorian restoration the hall is still splendid, and adorned with portraits, including two by Sir Peter Lely of Queen Henrietta Maria and General Monk. Exeter has had a mayor since the thirteenth century, when an earlier Guildhall existed, and not long after the first mayor of London; the two cities have had commercial links ever since.

Exeter has a fine example of an individual guild hall in Tuckers Hall, further along in Fore Street. It began as a chapel of the Fraternity of the Assumption of the Blessed Virgin Mary, alias the Guild of Weavers, Fullers (or Tuckers: the scourers and beaters in the final stages of woollen cloth-making) and Shearmen, among whose members would have been Sir Francis Drake's father. The cloth trade, started in the thirteenth century, provided a great deal of Devon's prosperity, in the manufacture of, at first, rough woollen cloth, later kersies (a lightweight worsted), and then serges, which continued until the eighteenth century. Celia Fiennes was amazed at the amount of cloth on sale in Exeter in the seventeenth century. The Weavers, Tuckers and Shearmen were thus a leading company. The religious fraternity was dissolved in the mid-sixteenth century and the chapel became the secular guild's meeting place. An upper floor was constructed, the barrel-vaulted roof plastered between the beams and the walls painted with frescoes, some of which remain behind the later seventeenth-century oak panelling. The woodwork is elaborately decorated with friezes of strapwork, grotesque masks, and the emblems of the guild, teasel frames, bales of cloth, bobbins and tucker's shears. One famous seventeenth-century Master was Thomas Crispin, born in Kingsbridge and founder of its grammar school. Today, as in the London livery companies, the "guild" members are Exeter businessmen who donate funds to maintain their fine hall and enjoy good dinners, sometimes inviting fellow liverymen from London companies, and endeavouring to keep up the old traditions.

Further on down Fore Street, The Mint is a narrow road leading to St Nicholas Priory. Although the large priory church was demolished after the Dissolution about 1536, an impressive range of buildings remains. When William of Normandy gave the church of St Olave's to Battle Abbey, the Benedictine monks who came to serve that church built the Priory. They used, in addition to the red sandstone breccia, some trap rock, and its contrasting rich brown makes a pleasing contrast set in a random pattern in the rough walls, particularly in the entrance hall, or Tudor Room, so called because of its decorated plaster ceiling. The Norman undercroft remains unchanged, its scalloped capitals and vaults divided by transverse arches. It is a miniature version of the crypt of Canterbury Cathedral, with the same peaceful atmosphere. On the first floor, reached by a graceful curved staircase, are the spacious Guest Hall, with a panelled screen, the Prior's Room and his study in the tower. The kitchen, with two great, probably thirteenth-century fireplaces, is like the Dartington Hall kitchen, although smaller. After the monks left, the Priory experienced centuries of use as a domestic residence before Exeter Corporation bought and restored it in 1913.

Fore Street descends steeply towards the river; on the left about two-thirds of the way down, West Street leads down to Quay Hill across the ring road. There is another medieval sandstone church, St Mary Steps, in West Street, with an exterior sixteenth-century clock below which in a niche sits Matthew the Miller with his two sons standing beside him. On the other side of the street is The House that Moved, a tall, four storeyed Elizabethan house that was moved on rollers when threatened with demolition in St Edmund Street in 1961. Immediately past St Mary Steps a narrow lane opens out to the left: Stepcote Hill, whose steep curve has shallow, worn steps up its right-hand side. It was once the main thoroughfare leading to the West Gate and the old bridge from the city centre. Surrounded now by roundabouts carrying the swirl of traffic converging on the new road bridges, several arches of the ruined and bombed medieval red sandstone bridge were repaired in 1977

by the City Council, and with a small ruined chapel make an oasis
with paths and lawns, a memorial like the shell of Charles Church
in Plymouth.

From Cricklepit Street leading into Quay Hill can be seen some
of the leat workings that fed the group of town mills once busy
here. Quay Hill winds down to the Quays where massive Victorian
warehouses accommodate part of the impressive Maritime
Museum, that commemorates Exeter's once considerable maritime
trade. Other parts of the museum lie across the canal, some moored
afloat. At the north end of the quay is the red-brick Custom House,
an elegant seventeenth-century building, with beautiful plaster
ceilings in the first-floor rooms, one particularly exuberant with
intertwined foliage, fruits and snakes hanging coiled as if about to
drop and sting drowsy excisemen into action.

With the exception of the clean red-brick lines of the University
of Exeter's mid-twentieth-century buildings on the northern edge
of the city, it cannot be said that the opportunities offered for new
architecture in the city by the clearance of war damage have been
seized upon in any impressive or beautiful way. But the prolifera-
tion of styles manage to exist relatively harmoniously together
despite all the ravages; and in addition to the buildings and
picturesque ruins, there are several delightful gardens and parks, to
form, with the Close, a green background for the predominant red
of the stone. Southernhay's elegant eighteenth-century crescent
was built on each side of the old town ditch, which about 1800 was
transformed into the lawns and gardens that flourish there today,
shaded by the massive ilex trees that grow luxuriantly in the south-
west.

On the north side of the city Northernhay Gardens, with palms
and exotic plants, incorporate a part of the Roman wall and adjoin
Rougemont House and Gardens; this house holds the archaeological museum and its gardens occupy the outer bailey of the
Norman Rougemont Castle, built, obviously, of red sandstone.
The gatehouse here is the only substantial remaining part of the
castle. The Roman wall continues west along the brow of the hill to
pass through Friernhay, an old, green, tree-shaded graveyard, and
then the curve of the wall's south-west corner is followed inside
by Bartholomew Terrace, whose Georgian porched and bow-
windowed houses have an inspiring view across the river valley to

wooded Haldon Hills. Even the moving red ruins of St Katherine's Almshouses off the south-east side of High Street offer seats in their small grassy garden.

One other feature in the city centre is especially interesting: Exeter's underground system was built to convey water, not traffic. The underground passages, reached at the east end of Southernhay, are a thirteenth-century network of aqueducts that brought water from a spring to the north of the city into the centre. The work was ordered by the dean and chapter, at first for the cathedral and then as a supply for the city. It is possible to walk for a quarter of a mile or so through the passages, whose strongly-built red walls are still in perfect condition. Here and there was previously a hole in the ceiling, a dipping hole, through which the citizens could draw water; most of the passages are high enough to walk upright in, and during the war they were used as safe air raid shelters.

Despite the road, rail and air traffic crowding into and out of the city, all the forms of trade and administrative activity of a county town, the large population, resident or commuting, Exeter offers many easily-reached viewpoints overlooking the great spaces to the south, and the gardens make it impossible to forget that here is the gateway and guardian of the greenest of counties.

Probably more than any other English county, Devon offers sites for all types of country house. Three were selected for great mansions in the generous sweeps of open country not far from Exeter. Killerton, to the north, was the home until recently of the Acland family. The present house is late eighteenth-century and used for conferences and holidays; the park is a West Country Westonbirt with a magnificent variety of trees.

Powderham Castle lies near the west bank of the Exe, south of Exeter. It is a large, battlemented, fortified mansion that was begun by Sir Philip Courtenay, Lord Lieutenant of Ireland, in the fifteenth century, and has remained the chief home of the Courtenays, Earls of Devon, ever since. The castle was enlarged and altered in the eighteenth century; it contains many fine paintings, several by Joshua Reynolds. Deer graze in the park where the huge old oaks give shade in summer and beautiful branch-forms in winter.

South-west of Powderham, near Chudleigh and the romantic wooded area around the limestone outcrop of Chudleigh Rocks, is

Ugbrooke House, the home since the sixteenth century of the Lords Clifford of Chudleigh. There was a house here as early as 1280, and a property on the site mentioned in documents from 1080. The present building, enlarged from a Tudor house, remnants of which remain, was designed by Robert Adam and built by the Lord Treasurer Clifford of the Cabal in 1760, to include a chapel where Roman Catholic mass is still regularly said. The house contains much of interest, including paintings of the family by Sir Peter Lely.

In the park is a grove of fine beech trees, "Dryden's Walk", where the poet is reputed to have finished his translation of Virgil while visiting the first Lord Clifford. Certainly the landscape has Virgilian tones, a pastoral setting that the twentieth century has miraculously done little to change.

HOLNE CHASE IRON AGE CAMP

The carriage-way folds a green band round the hill.
Tree-tops are at my feet. Below, the Dart
hisses through rocks and grips a promontory.
Alders aim at the sky, in conifer dark
a wren's voice cracks the quiet.
A path veins the hillside to the fort
where oaks within the bank's tonsure are gaunt
tall and barked with moss. An owl calls.
In this crown I feel a timewind
that eddies through skulls and dreams
to touch the hands that built these walls.

Wood and water for the fire and pot,
a hard haul up the hillside; the day's
round's filled with fish, flesh, fruit and root.
I weave a song into the rough frieze.
At dark we two make for the hut, lie
in warmth that's like a river of sun
streaming into the night. Then
a new life cries to break out of my life,
strongly driven on. A brief
peace we share, cradled and cradling again,
as shapes repeat on the hill, shawled in sun, rain.

Chapter Three

THE ROAD WEST – FROM ASHBURTON
TO PRINCETOWN

BOVEY TRACEY, ASHBURTON, Buckfastleigh, South Brent and
Ivybridge on the A38 are all jump-off points for Dartmoor. Except
for a sharp turn inward to avoid Bovey Tracey, the National Park
boundary follows the A38 from there as far as Ivybridge, where it
turns north-west to Lee Moor to continue northward. It runs just
east of Tavistock and on to Okehampton, thence eastward towards
Exeter, enclosing a total of 365 square miles. The southern lowland
areas of the park include some of the rich arable farmlands of the
South Hams, so that much of Devon's great variety of terrain is
enclosed within the park, and its *genius loci* offers an exhilarating
and ever-changing panorama.

Bovey Tracey is named after the river that passes through it to
join the River Teign near Chudleigh Knighton Heath; it is the only
remnant of the great heath that once covered the Bovey Basin, and
you can still hear nightingales sing there; and also after Henry de
Tracey who instituted a borough here in the thirteenth century.
There is a tradition that the church was built by Sir William de
Tracey to expiate his guilt for his part in the murder of St Thomas à
Becket in 1170.

From Bovey Tracey the A382 road runs north-west and leads
you through deep wooded Bovey Cleave and on over the moor to
Moretonhampstead, Manaton and Chagford, through areas rich in
prehistoric sites, and with medieval farms sheltered on the lower
slopes.

Further along the A38, Ashburton is a particularly pleasurable
small town. Its river is the little Ashburn that joins the Dart just
below Dart Bridge at Buckfastleigh. There was a Saxon settlement
in the Ashburn valley, and later the town grew up where the ancient
east–west route from Exeter westward crossed the Mariners' Way
that ran north–south from Barnstaple to Brixham. Although no
great estate grew up in the vicinity of Ashburton, it was to become

an important centre of trade, as the busiest of the stannary towns in the fifteenth and sixteenth centuries and as a wool-producing town for the cloth trade that grew up in the thirteenth and fourteenth centuries. The sheep-farmer's wool went to the cottage spinsters who sold it to the weavers, they in turn passed it on to a clothier or the fuller and perhaps dyer. The ubiquitous West Country surname Tucker is a synonym for fuller.

Other local industries were copper, ochre, umber, iron and arsenic mining on small scales, and the famous Ashburton marble was quarried until 1970. Ashburton pewter was of a high standard: it was a natural alloy to be worked here, being a blend of tin (the biggest component), copper, lead and antimony.

Ashburton, like Modbury, shows evidence of the great days of ecclesiastical life, in some of the old stones of its domestic architecture as well as the fine fifteenth-century church of St Nicholas. Good Bishop Stapeldon (1261?–1326), who became Lord Treasurer of the Realm and Professor of Canon Law at Oxford, where he founded Harts Hall and Stapeldon's Inn, the later Exeter College that has received many Devonians as students, and where his portrait hangs in the hall, provided a market and fair for Ashburton in 1310.

Today the visitor to Ashburton can enjoy the narrow streets with many slate-hung stone houses, a museum, shops and inns; if you are there in mid-June you will be offered a feast of music, art and crafts produced by the Ashburton Festival. It was inaugurated in 1980 to revive the town's ancient association with music and the arts, in memory of Bishop Stapeldon's chantry for choristers from 1314. The Ashburton Singers commissioned their conductor, Nicholas Marshall, to compose a cantata entitled *Even Such Is Time*, based on the life and poetry of Sir Walter Raleigh, Lord Warden of the Stannary Towns, of which Ashburton was one.

One of the most scenically beautiful roads in Devon leads up to the moor from Ashburton to Dartmeet, then on to the crossroads formed by the linking immediately east and west of Two Bridges of two pairs of conjoining roads: from Ashburton and Moreton-hampstead in the east, and from Tavistock and Yelverton in the west. The road to Yelverton and on to Plymouth goes through Princetown.

From Ashburton the road winds through low-lying wooded

country for a mile or so until it runs parallel with the east bank of the
Dart. This part of the Dart Valley is the most generously wooded
area in the whole of the National Park, consisting chiefly of broad-
leaved trees, oak, beech, ash, alder and some birch. The densely-
covered slopes and river banks are like a deep draught of green after
the dry open motor-road, only occasionally opening out into small
grass diamonds or triangles among the woodlands. At Holne
Bridge the road takes two right-angled turns to cross the river.
Holne derives from holly, one of the most common indigenous
evergreens of the region. The fifteenth-century bridge is built high
up above the river that here swirls tempestuously through a deep,
rocky channel, dark-brown and foaming. The narrow bridgeway
contains V-shaped refuges for pedestrians, originally to enable
them to escape being run down by pack-horses; now the absurd
weight of motor traffic it carries bears witness to the skill of the
medieval builders.

Now the road begins to climb, gently at first, still well-sheltered
by woods. A short way along on the right is the entrance to Holne
Chase Hotel, once a hunting lodge. The river makes a dramatic
horse-shoe loop here round the foot of a steep-sided promontory; a
track leads from the hotel around this hill, rising high above the
river, eventually rejoining the road above New Bridge. In their
struggle towards the sun, the trees nearer the river grow immensely
tall, and their tops incongruously reach to your feet as you walk.
Atop the end of this inland peninsula is Holne Chase Camp, a
perfectly circular earthwork with a single rampart and ditch,
probably late Iron Age. It must have afforded wide views when the
trees were kept felled, and a fine defensive position. In its centre the
crowns of thin tall silver birches and alder sigh of ancient
mysterious times.

On the west side of the promontory the Dart is augmented by the
East and West Webburn rivers whose confluence lies about a mile to
the north. The swift-flowing river provided a never-failing
water-supply and extra defence for the early settlers.

New Bridge is in fact another fifteenth-century structure, lower
and slightly narrower even than Holne Bridge. The flat, grassy
river bottom here is now a sizeable car park and starting point for
guided walks, and the site of a National Park information centre.
Flat rocks and paths along the river banks ensure its popularity, and

it is humming with activity all summer. Not only human: buzzards, whose numbers are increasing, swoop or hover, mewing, above, the green woodpecker laughs from his hiding-place, chaffinches forage for crumbs and the amphibious little dipper runs along the river-bed fishing, swims under or on the surface, and darts ashore to run along the rocks. Those are a favourite hopping ground for the acrobatic grey wagtail, whose extraordinary tail muscles operate like clockwork. The call of the nuthatch comes like a dog-whistle from its home in a lichen-covered oak, and the marsh tit exercises its voice on a variety of clear-pitched calls. Occasionally a dazzling turquoise kingfisher arrows along the river and is gone. In the calmer river pools near the banks companies of pond skaters in a variety of sizes gracefully swoop and figure-of-eight, hardly denting the surface of the water with their lightweight boots. In summer petrol-blue damsel-flies and great iridescent gold and green dragon-flies carry out their expert aerobatics all day long; it is a privilege when a dragon-fly alights on your arm or shoulder.

New Bridge and its immediate environs mark the dividing line between lowland and moorland conditions. The trees, except for an occasional holly and the hardy rowan that grows in the upland river valleys, stop here. Now the road winds steeply upward on to the moorland plateau, although this one follows the central lower area between the southern and northern heights. This is one reason for the views from along this route being so superb. From the first tor on the right of the road where it levels out there is a fine prospect back over Holne woods and the deep Dart cleave. Further along, as the road penetrates into the moor, comes the unfailing exhilaration of being in every way on top of the world. The view is of lofty rise upon rise, some smoothly whale-backed, some topped with the characteristic granite tors, from each one of whose irregularly-piled turrets is a different breathtaking view, and including landscape, cloudscape or distant glimpses of the sea. The vertical cracks, sometimes leading to caves inside the tors, invite legends about the hidden castles of ghostly huntsmen like the satanic leader of the Wish Hounds who hunt the moor in storms, although the cave-dwellers are generally no more sinister than rabbits or foxes or lost trampers sheltering from the rain or mist that can suddenly descend.

The tors are portions of the top of the granite batholith; after the molten magma had welled up from beneath the already formed sedimentary rocks and in turn cooled, it acquired a top covering of vegetation and soil; but where this was eroded by natural forces the top peaks of the granite were uncovered. The structure of the granite made it liable to horizontal and vertical cracks and joints, weaknesses easily penetrated by weathering forces that have broken down the rock. The varying sizes of the tors represent different extents of this weathering. Where there are fields of small granite rocks and stones, known as clatters, these are ruined tors.

In late summer the grey tors and the increasing cover of green bracken that now threaten to strangle much of the heather are still marvellously embroidered with the gold of gorse bloom and the pink and purple of ling, heath and bell heather. Yellow and mauve sounds an unlikely colour combination but in fact it is perfectly harmonious when worn by these native moorland plants. They are the most striking colours, but a closer look, particularly in August, reveals an astonishing variety of flora. In the numerous high valley bogs where the streams have their sources grow tiny, delicate species that you would think could not survive harsh winter conditions. The bog violet flowers early in the year, but its bright leaves and fruits flourish during the summer; the water crowfoot with its kidney-shaped leaves has a white flower like a very small buttercup; the shiny leaves of the marsh pennywort lie on the bright thick bog mosses whose varieties are almost legion, like the lichens. Bog pimpernel too creeps on the surface of the moss, its little flowers a delicate pink. Marsh St Johns Wort, with yellow flowers, cousin to the hedge variety, has pairs of rounded hairy leaves, while the ivy-leaved bell-flower is like a tiny Canterbury Bell. Two small aristocrats of this watery world are the bog asphodel, iris-leaved and yellow-flowered, and the bog bean whose leaves look like small broad-bean leaves and whose flower spikes rise above the water, the cluster of blooms pink outside and white inside, fringed inside with long white hairs. Two minute plants with innocent-sounding names are the sundew and the butterwort – but both are insec-tivores. The sundew's leaves, in a rosette lying on the ground, may be round or elongated. The leaves are covered with sticky bright red hairs which curve round and digest unwary flies and other small insects that settle on their attractive colour and are trapped. The white flowers grow at the top of long pink stems. The sundew is both exquisite and repellent, a species – that perhaps inspired John Wyndham to invent the triffid – that seems to trespass into a perverted function. The butterwort has modest violet-like flowers, but its leaves too are arranged in a basal rosette, and their edges roll inward to entrap insects.

The perfect time for making the acquaintance of all these extremely idiosyncratic plants is after rain, when the whole moor is thirst-quenched and refreshed, the streams sing in fortissimo on their way to the rivers, and all the colours of the vegetation are heightened with dewy, prismatic reflections. The grasses are decked with bright drops and the flowers open to the sun and light. Most of the valley bogs are safe to walk on with good boots and you can keep moderately dry by agile tussock-negotiating. It is only the deep mires, and the "feather beds" quilted with dazzling green, that can be perilous. People and ponies are said to have found their last resting-place in the feather beds, but in fact this has seldom happened, as far as is known.

On drier ground there is, besides heather and gorse, a common disreputable little plant, the dodder, that is a parasite living on gorse bushes; it has no roots or green leaves, only a maze of red or yellowish thread-like stems and clusters of pretty, pale-pink flowers. In contrast to these wicked little plants is the whortleberry (the bilberry of the north of England) or hurt. The moorfolk have always gone "picking hurts" every July and August, for pies and preserving; the berries are rich in vitamin C. The low-growing woody bushes grow high up sometimes among granite boulders, although they are found in the valley woods as well.

The old adage about kissing being in season when the gorse is in bloom, which it conveniently seems to be all the year round, is explained by the existence of two species of gorse: the common furze, that flowers in winter and spring, and the dwarf furze, flowering in summer and autumn.

The road to Princetown continues through the moorland village of Poundsgate; here the Devil, while on his way to claim a hostage out of Widecombe Church by means of a dreadful thunderstorm in 1638, stopped at the Tavistock Inn for a meal and paid the landlady with money that turned into dry leaves. Outside Poundsgate, the road runs over the high open moor for a couple of miles before the

precipitously winding descent to Dartmeet. The slopes above the
river here are a favourite feeding ground for ponies.

The Dartmoor pony is the most admired, most easily seen and
most discussed indigenous animal of the area. It is thought to be
descended from the prehistoric wild horses; like other native
breeds, these small hardy animals once roamed all over Britain, and
then were isolated in the wilder areas as civilization spread. Their
presence on Dartmoor, and the use made of them by man, has been
documented for almost a thousand years. The pure Dartmoor is
bay, black or brown, and stands about twelve and a half hands high,
a neat, strong, slim-legged pony with a bright, intelligent eye. But
cross-breeding through the introduction of alien stallions has
produced a wide range of variations, and quite a number of
skewbald and even grey ponies may now be seen, sought-after as
children's mounts, but as foreign to the moor as the Scottish black-
faced and Cheviot sheep, which graze here with the white-faced
and grey-faced native Dartmoors, or the striking Galloway cattle
with their white straitly-defined middle flanked by black bow and
stern, and the occasional group of picturesque Highlanders,
standing out against the red South Devons and South Hammers.

The ponies live in herds each with its stallion, although smaller
groups and individuals may be seen close to roads and car parks.
They have been fed by visitors in the past with disastrous results in
terms of accidents and health, but it is hoped that people are
learning to heed notices now; the ponies are not domesticated and
not at all averse to proving the quality of their teeth and hooves
when annoyed, although some may permit an occasional caress.
But although unbroken they are all owned, and rounded up each
autumn in "the drift", some to be sold and the rest released again.
They are always a delight to see, particularly after the charming
foals are born in spring and early summer, and their independent
hardiness is remarkable, few succumb to the blizzard conditions
that winter can bring, although in the hardest weather they shelter
in woods and valleys or go down into the lowlands and villages.

The other animal inhabitants of the moor are badgers, foxes,
otters, hares, rabbits (introduced centuries ago and encouraged to
breed in artificially made warrens for a food supply), voles, mice
and bats. It needs patience, quick eyesight and some expert
knowledge to catch sight of these shy creatures. Birds, butterflies

and insects are easier to find. On the high moor there are ravens as well as that ubiquitous and disreputable character, the carrion crow. The raven is easily recognized by its deep-throated croak, like a rusty chain being wound up, its lustrous shot-silk blue-black plumage and its size, almost as large as the buzzard. On a still day the smaller songbirds offset the savagery of the scavengers and the skylark seems to appreciate the wide views over the moor – and what more wonderful place could there be to listen to its soaring song?

Nearer the ground, slugs and snails are probably the commonest creatures of all in this well-watered region, as they are all over Devon, and the black slug grows to almost alarming proportions. One of the odder Dartmoor tales is of two reclusive ladies who lived at what is still called Snaily House, now in ruins, near Postbridge on the Two Bridges–Moretonhampstead road. It was known that they had no means of subsistence, yet when seen they appeared to be flourishing. Eventually some inquisitive villagers broke into the house when the two women were out and discovered no food at all but a black pot full of slugs: obviously the women's source of rich protein diet. But after their secret was out the two quickly pined away.

From Dartmeet, the confluence of the East and West Dart, the road again climbs steeply to the moortop and leads on three miles to Two Bridges, immediately south of the meeting of the Cowsic and West Dart rivers. This crossing marks roughly the centre of Dartmoor, although the northern section includes more remote and higher hills than the southern half. About two miles up the Dart is the point where Drake's Devonport leat was taken out and cut around the contours of the slopes and eventually down to Plymouth. It is possible to follow it for quite a distance. Nearer Two Bridges on the east bank of the Dart is Wistman's Wood. Like two other small upland copses, Piles Copse and Black Tor Beare, this is an oak wood where the small pedunculate variety of the tree grows among very large boulders, gnarled and with weirdly distorted branches like the trees in Arthur Rackham's pictures, clothed in lavish garments of ferns, mosses, lichens and flowering plants like wood sorrel and climbing corydalis. The roots and lower boles grow over and round the granite boulders to make strange sculptures in wood and stone.

Although these oak groves have led to the wilder fantasies of
those who have wrongly attributed all kinds of natural manifesta-
tion on Dartmoor to the Druids, this is undoubtedly one of the
most mysterious places on the moor; its sylvan aura is thick,
pervasive, slightly menacing, the plants and stones provocatively
promising yet withholding revelation. It has not yet been established how the three copses, in which some trees are 500 years old,
came to grow in these high valleys. Their native trees are as true
denizens of the place as the ponies, the gorse and the heather, in
contrast to the grim encroaching alien conifer plantations.

The natural scene, as everywhere else, is marked here by man.
The remarkable engineering of the leat is joined by particularly
strong moorstone walls dividing the upland pastures, the work of
the chain-gangs from Dartmoor Prison at Princetown, a little over
a mile further along the road to Yelverton. Princetown is a place of
archetypal grimness, of Dantesque gloom. Built on the open moor
over 1400 feet above sea level and exposed to all the elements, it has
over twice the rainfall of Plymouth, and more than its fair share of
fog and snow. The founder of this town, or rather village, was Sir
Thomas Tyrwhitt, Lord Warden of the Stannaries, who in 1780
began to reclaim land in this part of the moor, creating what he
hoped would be a successful moorland farming venture on his
estate at Tor Royal, half a mile south-east of Princetown, then
merely a group of cottages. In 1806 Tyrwhitt proposed that a prison
should be built on land acquired from the Prince of Wales as holder
of the Duchy of Cornwall, to which large parts of Dartmoor
belong. The prison was to house Napoleonic war prisoners (and
later American) previously incarcerated in hulks moored in the
Sound, before becoming the dreaded gaol for English convicts that
it still is today despite various plans for closure. Tyrwhitt had
discovered large stocks of good building granite near neighbouring
Hessary Tor and saw a supply of cheap labour rotting in the hulks.
The five original prison buildings, one of which still stands, were
built in blocks like the spokes of a wheel.

The prisoners were put to work quarrying granite and enclosing
fields. When the wars ended the prison closed until 1850, but
quarrying continued and Tyrwhitt had a rail-link built in 1823 to
transport the stone to Yelverton and Plymouth; this continued to
operate until the 1950s, in later years taking tourists to Princetown.

Today this is a disquieting place. Coaches and carloads of sightseers drive through to get a spine-chilling glimpse of the forbidding walls, or, despite road-signs near the prison enjoining "No stopping on this road", stop to peer, or visit the unattractive street, although the inns provide popular dancing and drinking. On one of the frequent days when mist or fog come down the great walls loom threateningly and you can indeed feel that here all hope has been abandoned. The houses along the straight street to incarceration are decaying, their soot-grey roughcast peeling, windows broken; along the path to the black-grey granite church built by American prisoners rainwater splatters from broken, hanging guttering. Inside, the cold bleakness is repeated despite good design and a wordy plaque commemorating Thomas Tyrwhitt, the progenitor of this dire place. But many prisoners are buried in the graveyard with no headstones to mark their cheerless resting places.

In the summer of 1982 a public exhibition of prisoners' paintings was mounted in a hall in Princetown village, a bleak building with doors that jammed, giving visitors a realistically imprisoned sensation. Many of the paintings were in bright colours that told of the artists' need to at least imagine places less uniformly grey. Princetown presents a sobering aspect of Dartmoor in total contrast to its idyllic side: the limitless views from Haytor, Brentor and countless other high points on fine days, the sheltered lushness of the river valleys, the snug farmsteads, and the peace and freedom of its grand spaces.

MICHELCOMBE LANE TO THE MOOR

Up is to light, space, the unknown:
under met branches the ground's muted,
the floor's rough and a granite block
midlane makes us diverge, clutches its crystals

winking an old cold eye at time and we,
like the flying ants on it, leave no mark
in the lane. We move though and see
perspectives through gates and meet lines

and angles. The lane ends at moorgate.
This vast is an element like love,
or the sea, that takes you into it,
wings you body and mind, then scares you,

throws a take-it-or-leave-it two-sided gift
of beauty and fear. You take it while you can.
Returning, the lane leads down
to the reclothing of leaves, tree-chasmed rivers,

arable coloured curves, the little towns;
the endless secret ways of lanes and minds.
Seen clearer through eyes washed in space,
the liberating sea of the high moor.

Chapter Four

DARTMOOR – THE GREAT SOURCE

DARTMOOR IS THE largest of the granite vertebrae of the South-West. The gigantic geological processes that left the heather- and gorse-covered tor-topped heights we admire today made it a huge repository of valuable elements and minerals: water, tin and other ores, china clay, and suitable conditions for nurturing hardy farmstock and conifer forests.

The National Park was formally established in 1951. Ian Mercer, the National Park Officer, has called it a place where we retain the illusion of wilderness, and if all the organizations and groups active on the moor are noted it seems amazing that even an illusion can still be experienced. But it can, and it is no illusion that people are still lost or die of exposure on Dartmoor. None the less it is a wilderness to which one is irresistibly drawn, by both love and respect.

Man's first tentative settlement of Dartmoor was made by Mesolithic hunters in about 8000 BC. They penetrated the birch forests that covered the moor after a temperate climate had replaced the last cold phase of the Ice Age. Clearance slowly progressed with burning of the woodlands during the next millennia; as some of the surviving trees decayed, peat began to form about 3000BC.

Around 2000 BC the Bronze Age Beaker People crossed the Channel from Western Europe and settled the moor in quite large numbers; they remained in possession of it for a couple of thousand years, until the Iron Age Celts largely replaced them.

Apart from a few Stone Age tombs it is the Bronze Age stone rows, circles and standing stones, and almost 2000 hut circles, also numbers of walls marking their field system, that give us a vivid impression of these people. When they were living on Dartmoor the climate was much milder than it is now.

The greatest surviving concentrations of Bronze Age monuments are in the river valleys that drop down from the south and south-west of the high moorland plateau from their sources in the peat bogs. From the time when a sprinkling of Palaeolithic people lived in Devon we can experience a historic span of 22,000 years to bring us to our own century by walking, for instance, down the Erme Valley to Ivybridge, passing Beaker People settlements on Brown Heath and Erme Pound, in which area are also stone rows, cairns and cists. The ancient burial places yielded the finds that the past century of scientific archaeological exploration has made, that enable us to picture something of the domestic and daily life of these people. The finds include pottery with distinctive decoration, whetstones, arrow-heads, scrapers, daggers, axe-heads and spindle-whorls.

We may never know the exact significance of the stone rows, and stone circles like those at Scorhill, near Gidleigh, and Grey Wethers to the north of Postbridge and west of Fernworthy Forest, and the single tall freestanding stones, which can be as high as nine feet. At Drizzlecombe, above Sheepstor near Meavy in the Plym Valley, there are three, one of which is particularly impressive, and connected with stone rows. The whole of this area is a Bronze Age sanctuary with several barrows and cists.

As the Beaker People had no written language it will probably never be known what their beliefs and ideas were in relation to their powerful monuments. But although their lives must have been short and probably brutish, their perseverance in moving and setting up huge blocks of stone for a purpose other than the purely practical at least reveals great imagination, even if it was only stimulated by fear. Admittedly they are crude compared with the Pyramids, constructed within more or less the same cultural period; to me they are in their inscrutability even more impressive.

The Celts of the Iron Age came from northern Europe and lived on the moor from 500 BC, through the Roman occupation which did not penetrate far into Dartmoor, and were then subjugated by the Saxons, who came during the seventh century and completed the colonization of Devon. The climate deteriorated during the Iron Age period, and people gave up living on the high moor. The Celts built the chain of hill forts that circle the southern edge of the moor and are all in well-picked defensive sites. In the Dart Valley are Hembury Castle above Buckfast Abbey, and Holme Chase Camp. In the Teign Valley are three magnificent Iron Age castles, Cranbrook and Prestonbury on either side of the river, and Wooston lower down.

The Saxons lived during a period when the climate was improving, and created large estates around the edges of the moor. They built the first churches and villages in stone rather than wood. It was not until after the Norman conquest that the warmer climate induced people to settle the higher parts of the moor again, and then chiefly to work rather than live. Recently much work has been carried out on the ruined medieval village at Houndtor, south-west of Manaton, one of the higher settlements. Quite near here, north of Widecombe and near the road from there that joins the Moretonhampstead–Two Bridges road, is Grimspound, a well-preserved Bronze Age settlement, an enclosed village, unfortified but with substantial remains of twenty-four huts, some with a windbreak made by a curving stone entrance passage-way, and traces of raised stone beds and cooking stones.

The ancient moormen travelled from settlement to settlement. They used the ridgeways to and from the coast to trade abroad or perhaps to take their cattle to summer pasture when the marshes around the river deltas were drier and the grass good. But the earliest documented Dartmoor tracks are the lychpaths leading across the moor to Lydford where all the moor people had to bury their dead until Bishop Bronescombe gave permission for people in the east part of the moor to use Widecombe church. This custom of taking the body by horse and cart across the moor was still in use in the 1930s. It was far more wearisome than the journey the people of Kingsbridge made to carry their dead to Churchstow, or that made by Salcombe folk to Malborough.

The monks from Buckfast, Buckland, Plympton and Tavistock used paths between their abbeys across the moor, often marked by stone crosses, some of which remain. Parts of the Abbot's Way are easily reached from the Avon Dam. The moorland rivers were spanned in medieval times by clapper bridges made with huge flat slabs of granite wide enough for pack-horses and small carts. A fine example is at Postbridge.

The Normans declared Dartmoor a royal forest for hunting, with rights for the commoners to graze their stock which have never been lost. Proper roads were slow in coming, and it was only by 1780 that a turnpike road was built from Plymouth to Tavistock, and thence to Moretonhampstead. But the moor wears an intricate web of tracks ancient and modern made by many categories of traveller: pony and sheep tracks, tinners' paths, farmers' and peat-cutters', and ramblers' tracks to particular points of interest, like the letter-box at Cranmere Pool north of Postbridge, and the many other letter-boxes that have sprung up; and there are traces of several small railways for particular industrial purposes, like that from Princetown to Plymouth and the granite railway at Haytor built by George Templer to transport granite from his quarries for the building of the British Museum, the National Gallery, London Bridge and other projects.

All along the edges of the moor, at the end of deep steep lanes, are moorgates, five-barred gates that mark the end of tarred roads and where motorists must get out and walk, over the moor or to see the views. The fine-woven network of lanes is as characteristic of Devon as the moor itself or the rocky coastline. It was created by the Saxons who cleared the fertile lowlands of trees and scrub and made the small fields with their angular shapes by banking and hedging them into the many small holdings that still remain. The banks were built into a U-shape with stones cleared from the fields, and soil, and planted with trees for shelter and firewood. The field hedgebanks are not generally very high and most have lost their trees. But the lanes, some original boundaries, have in many places been so deeply eroded by the traffic of centuries that the banks can be up to twenty feet high, green tunnels whose roofs are interlaced branches. It is fascinating to nose one's way through them and come upon sudden stunning views through gateways. Even though the view may be partly spoiled by a large metal barn clamped on a rise or even on the moor itself it is almost always a revelation. It is not always easy for individual land-owners, the National Park Authority, the industrialists and the military who control large areas in the north of the moor, to live in harmony together, but they succeed reasonably well.

As well as the largest, farming is also the oldest industry on the moor. Ian Mercer put it neatly when he said that farming began when Neolithic man realized that it was more sensible if you rounded up and domesticated the long-haired wild cattle instead of throwing stones at them. He built his stockpens for cattle, primitive sheep and pigs, out of the plentiful supplies of moor-stone and grazed his stock on the hills that he had cleared of trees;

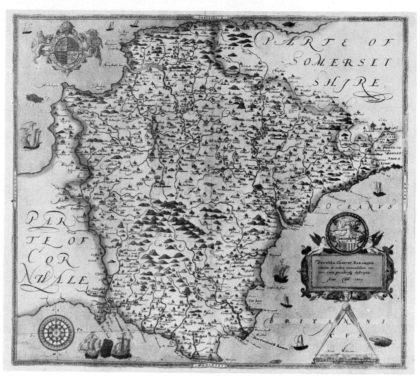

Saxton's Map of Devon, 1575

Exeter Cathedral Close

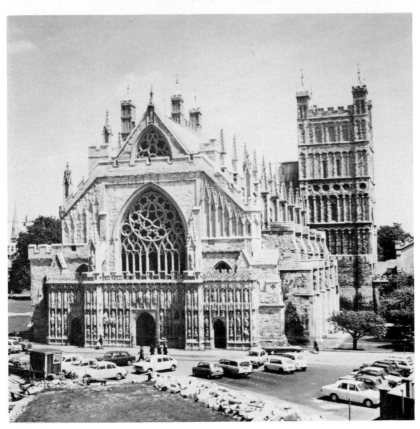

Exeter Cathedral

Totnes Castle

Bowerman's Nose, Dartmoor

Hanger Farm, Cornwood

Hexworthy Bridge

Widecombe-in-the-Moo

there has been stock-farming ever since except in the worst climate eras.

In the relatively good climate of the Bronze Age man was able to divide parts of the moor into long strips for cultivation, as remaining walls show. Later Saxon lynchets, terrace-like strips that were cultivated land, are found in a few higher areas with good soil.

The Saxons, like the Celts before them, knew how to choose good sites for their farms on the edges of the moor. They are on southward-facing slopes sheltered from the prevailing south-west winds and near water, never hard to find in a region rich in rivers and springs. One example of an ancient farm on the moor's edge is Hanger Farm near Cornwood, which was established in early medieval times, like Fardel Manor and Cholwich Farm higher to the west on Lee Moor. Hanger is beautifully situated on a sheltered slope overlooking the trees of Blachford Park and Cornwood Parish. The present house was built as a prosperous yeoman's home and later extended as befitted a gentleman's residence. The granite ashlar walls are immensely thick, there are massive fireplaces of moulded granite, one with a wooden lintel, stone flags on the floors and medieval stone window frames with iron bars. During the eighteenth century Hanger was renovated and furnished with decorative plaster work in the form of a moulded circular panel in the charming drawing-room, whose walls are also panelled.

The birch and willow groves of post-Ice Age Dartmoor were joined by pine, hazel and deciduous oak. When the bogs formed on the central plateau the trees could grow only below the edges of the moor and in the river valleys, although from the eighteenth century onwards beeches were planted in copses and other trees tried out to serve as windbreaks fairly high up, but not very successfully.

But it was not until the late eighteenth century that tree-planting was undertaken seriously on Dartmoor. The Duchy of Cornwall began to plant conifer in a small way in mid-century. Then after World War One the newly-established Forestry Commission advised planting 5000 acres of moorland, as a work-providing measure and to grow timber. Sitka spruce, native to Alaska, was the advised species for the bleak moorland areas, it is a quick-growing, handsome, straight pine that can tolerate cold, wet and icy conditions, and is ready for use in twenty years. The

Commission now manages about four and a half thousand acres in
the National Park and more at Exeter Forest.

The documented industrial history of Dartmoor began in the twelfth
century when tin was discovered, first in the Plym valley, then in
other places. (It had been worked in a small way long before this.) For
half a century Dartmoor became the largest tin-producing area in
Europe. The tin rush was quickly controlled by elaborate and strict
laws which remained in force until the nineteenth century. When a
tinner discovered ore, at first as "stream tin", the mineral stones and
gravel washed down from the parent lode by the action of water, and
forming a "stream" which could be several yards deep, and later as a
deep lode mined by shaft, he could mark out either his stream works
or his mine. After extracting the ore by digging and washing it was
smelted at the "blowing-house", a granite furnace heated by charcoal
and fanned by bellows worked by a water wheel. The molten metal
was poured into granite moulds producing blocks of the finest white
tin weighing 200 or 300 lb. The tin was graded for quality and
recorded in the blowing-house book. Then it was stamped at the
stannary town before sale.

The Dartmoor tinning region was divided into four stannaries
based on Chagford, Tavistock, Ashburton and Plympton. They
held their own Parliament, to legislate, hold trials and impose
sentences for abuses of the laws. The bounds of the four stannaries
met in the heart of the moor at Crockern Tor, near Two Bridges, and
it was here that the "Parliament" of almost a hundred members,
convened by a warden who officiated from as early as 1198, met. A
reminder of the summary harshness of the law exists in the square
keep of grim Lydford Castle prison where sentenced miners were
held or hanged. William Browne, the Tavistock poet, wrote of it:

> I oft have heard of Lydford law,
> How in the morn they hang and draw,
> And sit in judgment after.

The miners have left evidence of their labours in ruined blowing-
houses, old mine shafts and great heaps of stones near the streams in
which they were washed.

The moor did not yield its bounty willingly, and it was a brutally
hard life for the miners, who also lost much of their profits to early

entrepreneurs. They toiled on the surface in terrible weather, or in the adits at their peril, for long hours with the crudest of wooden tools. Their emblem, the three entwined tinners' rabbits, symbolized their burrowing kinship with the rabbits reared by the warreners. But the linked rabbits, seen beautifully carved in wood on roof bosses in Ugborough and Widecombe churches, were also an older emblem from pagan times, a fertility symbol like the sow and her litter who can also be seen at Ugborough church.

The quarrying of granite on Dartmoor has continued for centuries and the Merrivale quarry is operating today on the site of ancient workings. The old buildings of Devon are so attractive because they are built of indigenous material: stone, slate, cob and thatch. It is often possible to find the small quarry that supplied limestone, sandstone or slate at a stone's throw from the house it grew into. Most of the once numerous quarries are now disused, but about ten large ones still work on the extraction of granite and limestone.

The industry that has scarred the moorscape more than anything else is china clay. Although William Cookworthy first discovered china clay in Cornwall and founded his operations in the larger pits there, the Lee Moor works east of the river Erme began extracting clay about 1840. The great white conical waste tip mountains were a familiar and not unbeautiful landmark against the purple-blue moors until recently, when they were "topped" for safety and to reduce their size.

The basic element in china clay was formed out of the feldspar in granite having been decomposed by immensely hot steam and gases and transformed into kaolinite. The extraction process is now fully mechanized and requires only a small workforce. The slurry that has been washed down is taken up the hillside from the pit through a long pipe and then subjected to various washing, heating and drying treatments to extract the pure kaolinite and make it into easily transportable pellets for lorry shipment. It is used in paper, ceramics, plastics, rubber, paint, textile and other industries.

Although the landscape for a mile or so around the claypits is powdered with white dust, there is a firm policy now for all quarrying firms to reduce damage to landscape and make good as far as possible. Waste material, particularly the overburden, is used to create banks to hide the workings; grass, trees or other plants are planted on banksides, infilling is carried out. The quarriers try to minimize noise, dust, wear and tear by washing lorry wheels, enclosing plant and erecting banks.

The ball clay pits in the Bovey Basin are extensive. Ball clay is called after the method first used to extract it: workers dug out the clay by hand with "thirting spades", tubils (or twybills, double-ended bills, with an axe blade on one side and a mattock on the other), lumpers, and pogs. A pog was a metal spike attached to a long wooden handle, rather like the tool park-keepers use to pick up waste paper. The tubil was designed to cut the clay into roughly rectangular lumps called "balls". Now the endearingly named tools can be seen only in the Finch Foundry Museum at Sticklepath, and the clay is dug by mechanical earth-grabbers that dump it into trucks for transport to the storing sheds where the various grades are sorted before being shredded, dried, pulverized, mechanically bagged and packed on wooden pallets.

Most of the ball clay is situated just below the earth's surface. It lies in slanting bands interspersed by narrower strips of lignite, and the cut sides of the wide shallow pits make pleasing patterns. Ball clay was formed by being washed out of the Dartmoor granite by the natural action of rivers and streams and deposited elsewhere by sedimentation, whereas china clay remained close to its area of origin.

Ball clay is more plastic than china clay, useful in making insulators, and a multitude of other artefacts developed since the making of the first humble clay pipes used since Roman times. The processed product is transported by road and rail and through the port of Teignmouth nearby. Now it is taken the five miles there by heavy truck, but between 1793 and 1939 the clay balls, each weighing about thirty-six pounds, were loaded into barges and pulled manually along the Stover Canal to where it joined the tidal Teign at Newton Abbot. James Stover built the canal which was also used by his son George to carry granite from the Haytor quarries, brought to the canal along his railway made of granite sets.

There is now a new extractive project afoot for which plans and forebodings are developing fast. It has long been known that there were resources of tungsten in South Devon. Recently it was confirmed that substantial quantities of it lie beneath Crownhill

Down, one of the closest open areas to Plymouth on its north-east boundary, and not far from Dartmoor National Park. Tungsten (a Swedish word meaning heavy stone) is a relatively rare steel-grey heavy metallic element, a native compound of the salt of tungstic acid, or iron, and manganese. It is used for making lamp filaments and alloying high-speed steel. As world supplies are short it seems all too likely that the Crownhill plans will go ahead and the dumping of vast amounts of waste material inevitable in this type of extraction will violate the landscape far more than even china and ball clay working.

Despite the vastly increased traffic of recent years Dartmoor is still the perfect place for walking. People have been rambling here for almost two centuries. One of the earliest to record her delight in it was Sophie Dixon, who died at Plymstock in 1858. She wrote a journal of her excursions on Dartmoor, published at Plymouth in 1830. At that time she was living at Princetown, from where the expeditions set off. She and her companions were very energetic, rising at 4 or 5 a.m. every day, and once at 1 a.m., to get the best of the summer morning hours. They walked on average thirty miles a day, and covered a hundred miles in four days. Sophie also wrote poems that show how well she knew every aspect of the moor; in one poem she notes that some sunsets "give to every rock and peak, the semblance of perfect transparency".

To be on Dartmoor uplifts in every way, at every time and season: when spring brings the first delicate plant growth and sunshine to the stern outlines, when summer allows the moor to stretch and bask, a paradise for all the living creatures that seek it; when autumn brings rich colours and scents to cleaves and hills, and when winter obliterates landmarks and declares the dangerous forces of nature strongest; and at night under moon and stars its shadowy whale-backed slopes breathe like supermundane beings impervious to the swarming life that scratches their surface.

OLD BANTHAM

Tides flood in and out at six knots,
make huge waves in the sand
that stretches mile-gold flats at low,
firm ground for bird and man.

Upover the Ham breakers roar.
Here in the river the current
flexes its power twice in the day,
shrugging off weight of water. Spent

shrimps and crabs wait in the pools
for oystercatchers' snatches, green
weeds are deftly lifted by
lightfoot turnstones. Old heron

hunches his ruff against the breeze,
flies creaking off at our coming.
Two men fall about laughing, muddy,
high up the estuary, catching

fish by hand. A century gone
salmon were twopence a pound and good,
so here three friends could dine well
for a tanner, with cider from the wood.

Chapter Five

FLOODS THAT TO THE SEA FLOW

THE GREAT PEAT sponge of the central Dartmoor bogs was long ago hailed as "the mother of manie rivers". Of the twelve chief rivers, only two, the Taw and the Torridge, run to the north coast; the other ten, with their numerous, sometimes considerable, tributaries, all make their way through our region to the English Channel; and eight of these rise on Dartmoor: Teign, Dart, Avon, Erme, Yealm, Plym, Meavy and Tavy. The remaining two almost sever the south-west peninsula at the east and west boundaries of Devon: the Exe has its source on Exmoor, and the Tamar, that marks the county boundary between Devon and Cornwall for much of its length, rises in Cornwall four miles east of Morwenstow on the north coast south of Hartland Point.

This rich fount of rivers makes Devon an especially well-watered region, except during severe drought. They keep it lush and green, tend its vegetation, crops, flora, and fauna with their generous streams, speak to its acres with their "choral multitudes", the "cry" that can be mysterious, alluring or sinister – the old jingle, "River Dart, River Dart, every year thou claim'st a heart", points to the formidable aspect of floods in spate, and dangerous, unpredictable natural forces.

The lengths of the main arteries vary: the longest river is the Exe, with seventy miles, followed by the sixty-mile-long Tamar and forty-five-mile-long Dart. Smaller but equally beautiful estuaried rivers like Erme and Yealm run for only fourteen and twelve miles; but even the little Gara, John Masefield's trout-stream at Slapton, meanders through almost ten miles of remote South Hams countryside; and the innumerable tributaries and streams provide the presence of running water in every acre. Springs are equally ubiquitous; yet, apart from in the moorland bogs, the good drainage conditions, natural or man-made, prevent waterlogging in all but a few low-lying marshy places now jealously conserved as natual habitats.

From their headwaters on the high moor the young rivers move at a cautious pace at first over the granite plateau, but take sudden and often sharp tumbles into their cleaves and valleys at the moor's edge, cascading among huge granite boulders and cutting deep fissures in the rocks, activity enforced on them by a tilting of the terrain away from their inclinations. The steep rocky valley sides of all the rivers are thickly treed in many places, as in the Dart Valley. Dart is in fact an old English word meaning "oak tree", so the river was called after the trees that lined its banksides; and presumably Dartmoor was so called at the period when the oak and other broad-leaved species grew on the moor.

As they descend into lower country the rivers flow calmly at times through wider channels, although when they again narrow even quite low down there are rocky, white-capped patches. On the whole their waters are clean, often peaty-brown; the Yealm's proximity to the china-clay workings at one time turned it opaque and milky, and farmers and factories can still cause some pollution. But only rarely now are fish poisoned; and the thirty-five river wardens of the South-west Water Authority patrol every yard of the rivers every year, on the watch for polluters and poachers.

The estuaries of the Exe, Teign, Dart, Plym and Tamar, and the Salcombe–Kingsbridge ria, are all wide enough to accommodate shipping, particularly the Plymouth rivers. So many ideal harbours for the smaller ships of the past inevitably made Devon the cradle of the sea-dogs, and its savage coastline served to sharpen their maritime teeth. Now the smallboat sailors and canoeists find paradise in the estuaries with their tricky veering breezes whipping out of the valleys, and their rocky rapids upstream.

From a few miles down from the Exe's source at The Chains, a lonely area of Exmoor, it is possible to follow much of the river's course to Exeter from the parallel-running A396 road. After about twenty-five miles the river crosses the Somerset–Devon border south of Dulverton. The Exe Valley then runs almost due north-south to Exeter, in beautiful, often thickly wooded unspoilt country, through cleaves and pasture-lands, past idyllic villages and ancient settlements. It passes through the old cloth-making centre of Tiverton fifteen miles from Exeter. A few miles further along, Cadbury Castle, an Iron Age fortification on the New Red

Sandstone hill, offers one of the most superb views in Devon, of Exmoor and Dartmoor and often the distant blue hills of Somerset and Cornwall beyond.

At Exeter, the river, after having been confined between quite narrow walls for centuries, has been widened again to flow smoothly without danger of flooding under the new motor-road bridges. (On the south side of the city it is spanned by an immense bridge a few miles before the end of the M5, that after the bridge cuts through dramatically excavated steep red sandstone earth walls.)

Near Custom House Quay, a hundred yards south of the bridges in an overgrown area that still contains the old mill-leats taken from the river, is the end of the Exeter ship canal whose inlet is opposite Topsham, and which still functions. It was built in the sixteenth century after the Courtenay family of Powderham Castle opposite Topsham had built weirs across the river, at what became known as Countess Wear after Countess Isabella de Fortibus, in order to force ships to discharge their cargo and pay revenue at the Courtenay-owned port of Topsham. It is comical to see small freighters gliding through the level water-meadows on their way to and from Exeter.

Three miles from the city along a straight Roman road, the little town of Topsham lies on a promontory on the east bank of the Exe, where the estuary starts to open out to over one mile across. At low tide its mudflats are a feeding ground for many species of water-birds. Topsham was used by the Romans as a coastal port for Exeter, their Isca Dumnoniorum, and was then busy again in the thirteenth century, when Purbeck stone was unloaded at its quay and carted to Exeter for building enlargements to the Cathedral. Leland wrote: "Heere is the great trade-rode for shippes that usith this haven: and especially for the shippes and marchant mennes goodes of Excester."

The additional trade brought to Topsham by the closing of the river was an advantage, although it remained a compact small town, an ideal size for a community that still lives happily in its charming houses, and has only been developed in quite a small way to the north, apart from one brash block of flats near the waterfront. The main Exeter–Exmouth road bypasses the town to cross the bridge over the Clyst, and it is a sudden entry into the past to turn into Topsham. I was there on a cold October Saturday afternoon after a shower had left roads and roofs swept and shining, and walking along the famous street called Strand discovered the Topsham Museum open and its founder, Dorothy Holman, receiving visitors.

Topsham vied with Dartmouth as a shipbuilding town in medieval times and supplied ships for combating the Armada and for the Napoleonic wars. It traded woollen goods from Exeter for fruit and wines, and joined in the Newfoundland fishing trade. Dorothy Holman's forebears were shipbuilders and master mariners; John Holman, who founded the family firm, was born in 1800, of a line already long in seafaring experience. Under his eagle eye the firm flourished, and built fine brigs, yachts, three-masted schooners, ketches and barques. He constructed a covered yard, a dry dock and extensive offices. The sail-loft was in Miss Holman's present elegant home. The little town was very different then: chaotically busy and noisy with the work of saw-mills, nail-shops, rope-walks, smiths and shipwrights. On the river side of the Strand were all the quays, yards and some workshops, where now are gardens. Old maps show the narrow garden plots behind the houses as at Totnes, Modbury and Kingsbridge, and then gradually extended late seventeenth- and early eighteenth-century merchants' houses with their gable ends to the street. Here are the "Dutch" houses with their curved gables. Each one is different and the street is a joy to explore. Topsham merchants traded woollen goods in Holland and probably brought back the architectural fashion together with the bricks with which they ballasted their empty ships on the homeward voyage. But the local touch given to the Renaissance style is unique. The houses have side courtyards within high gateways, wide, elegant staircases, and in some cases panelling and plastered ceilings. Some have underground passages, escape routes for smugglers, with a network of interconnecting boltholes and tunnels at the back of the Strand houses.

After shipbuilding came to an end at the turn of the century, the Holmans took their shipping interests to London, but Dorothy returned to her house, No. 25 Strand, and built up the museum, housed in the old sail-loft on the first floor, with a fine polished wood floor.

George Gissing wrote of Topsham in *The Private Papers of Henry Ryecroft*, as "one of the most restful spots I know". He liked to sit on the red sandstone terrace on which stands the parish church of St

Margaret, watching the evening tide coming up the broad estuary full of boats and birds, after his long rambles on each side of the estuary. There is still a ferry that runs to Starcross opposite. Then after the space and freshness of the estuary country, a drink would be the obvious pleasure at one of the various handsome old inns that echo with the voices of merchants and sailors from the time when Topsham dealt with all the maritime trade of Exeter.

The broad lower reaches of the Exe estuary, surrounded by the warm sandstone reds of gently rolling landscape, are made almost into a lake with its narrow entrance from the sea formed by the crook'd sandy finger of Dawlish Warren opposite The Point, at Exmouth, swirling with perilous currents. Exmouth, on the east side, is the earliest established seaside resort of Devon and the first town westward with sand beaches. Although the old shipbuilding and customs port was overrun by dull Victorian development, there are some attractive spots still, early Victorian houses on the Beacon and in Bicton Street and Louisa Terrace. Dawlish Warren is best in winter, when the campsite is quiet and the bird sanctuary on the Warren end comes into its own, surrounded by wild winds and seas and blowing sand and spray. Although the visiting summer birds are interesting, even more so are the great winter flocks of dunlin, Brent geese and widgeon, with sometimes elegant black and white suited avocets from Africa with their long delicate upward-curved elastic bills and warning cry that has earned them the decidedly inelegant name of "yelper". Another rarity of Dawlish Warren is the sand crocus, found only here in Britain.

The neighbouring river west of the Exe is the Teign. Exe means "water", Teign, "stream", while ubiquitous Avon is Celtic for "river", and Meavy probably means "sea-gull river". The Teign is a twin-headed river, the North Teign rises at Teignhead near Quintin's Man and below Whitehorse Hill a mile south-east of Cranmere Pool, while South Teign's source is just south-east of the mysterious Grey Wethers stone circle. It runs through the Forestry Commission Fernworthy conifer forest, to be lost in Fernworthy Reservoir, made by damming the river valley here. Several farms, antiquities and two bridges were inundated despite protesters' cries, and only briefly after drought do they reappear. The twin branches converge at Leigh Bridge in woods in which the North

Teign has already been clothed for several miles of its beautiful valley, and continue to pass through the moorland stannary and market town of Chagford, "gorse ford", and under its medieval bridge. The parish contains a section of moorland, including the area around Batworthy where there was an extensive prehistoric settlement, marked by hut-circles, stone rows and standing stones, and the rock basin on Kes Tor. The road to the moor here ends in a wild scatter of great boulders above the steep slope to the river.

Below Gidleigh Common there is a clapper bridge where the Walla Brook joins the North Teign; this is the second bridge on this river, the first is below ruined Teignhead farm. Just above the river, torrential here even though still small, and immediately below Scorhill with its stone circle, is a *tolmen*, a "holed" stone. If you believe in fertility rites you must risk a splashing to crawl through the hole.

Up to about ten miles beyond Chagford the Teigns have run east and slightly north, until at Clifford Bridge the river takes a southward direction and from Dunsford runs almost directly south to the start of its estuary at Newton Abbot.

One of the most beautiful of Devonshire river bridges is Fingle Bridge, reached by footpaths from Chagford. The bridge is probably sixteenth-century, spanning the river that runs for miles here through its densely-wooded steep-sided cleave. On each side of Fingle Bridge are the magnificent ancient hilltop Iron Age forts, Cranbrook and Prestonbury Castles, with Wooston lower down river. The views from them are more than worth the effort of gaining their heights, to the moorland stretching away and away, down to the green welcome of the lowlands. A castle of quite another kind lies at the end of a high promontory, visible from near Fingle Bridge: Castle Drogo, the twentieth-century granite palace built by Sir Edwin Lutyens for Julius Drewe, who made his fortune from the Home & Colonial Stores. It is heavy and stark, but as successful in its image as Lutyens' houses always were.

The vegetation of this long wooded valley is particularly exuberant: among the many ferns of Devon, perhaps it is the delicate lime-green harts' tongue with its violin-shaped opening fronds, and the great palm-like king fern, that are the most typical. One of the most luxuriant displays of wild daffodils in Devon greets the spring in the Dunsford Wood nature reserve, and all along the wooded valley primroses, wood anemones and bluebells glow unfailingly each year.

Past villages, ancient farms and houses, every one intensely confident in its own persona – Dunsford, Doddiscombsleigh, Christow, Canonteign, a recently restored Elizabethan mansion, Chudleigh near a dramatic outcrop of limestone rock, Chudleigh Knighton Heath of the nightingales; past the Heathfield ball clay pits the river flows, to circle the race-course at Newton Abbot and open out into its estuary, considerable although less broad than Exe, its mouth, too, between the bridge-linked towns of Shaldon and Teignmouth, almost enclosed by a sand spit's curved finger. Here it is on the east side, and vivid crimson instead of the gold of Dawlish Warren.

Newton Abbot is a large modern town, once a little twelfth-century settlement. Little is to be seen of the old town now, although Bradley Manor, to the south-west, is a fine fifteenth-century house. But a mile or two past Newton Abbot on the road to Shaldon is the hamlet of Haccombe, consisting of a couple of farms and a mansion, and one of the most perfect Early English churches in existence. The red sandstone here is a light-coloured rubble and the little church is pinkish-grey. It was built by Sir Stephen de Haccombe after his return from the Crusades in 1233 and dedicated unusually to St Blaise. It has four exceptionally fascinating features, its tombs and brasses, stained glass, curious "vested" arms, and floor tiles.

The tombs include four striking effigies. One is of Isabella de Haccombe, who died in 1341, wearing a graceful long mantle and holding a missal. Life-size Sir Hugh Courtenay and his wife Philippa, early fifteenth-century, lie on a high table tomb of Beer Stone. Beside them is the most beautiful of the figures. It is in miniature, carved of alabaster, and thought to commemorate Edward, eldest child and only son of Sir Hugh and Lady Philippa, who probably died at Oxford at the age of sixteen. His effigy is an example of a Heart Tomb, so called after the practice of burying the heart and body in different places. This diminutive figure is extraordinarily moving; and his dress is a wonderful example of medieval fashion: he wears a jupon ornamented down the chest with quatrefoils and with a scalloped edge, and a heavy belt.

The church has five interesting brasses on the nave floor. Sir Nicholas Carew, nobly formidable, who died in 1469, wears fifteenth-century armour and holds a huge two-handed sword. Thomas Carew, who died in 1586, it is thought of gaol fever contracted at the "Black Assize", wears sixteenth-century plate armour. His wife Maria, who died in 1589, is in formal Elizabethan dress. Elizabeth Carew died in 1611, and Thomas Carew and his wife Anne in 1676 within two days of each other.

The expressions on all the faces are vivid and varied and the details of wrinkles on the brows, hair and moustache remarkable. In the brass to Thomas and Anne the style becomes less refined but strongly baroque and macabre, decorated with skulls, bones and hour-glasses, as well as what appear to be the tools of the ball clay industry. Beneath them is an inscription with their names and dates and a verse:

> Two bodies ly beneath this stone
> Whom love and marriage long made one
> One soyle conioynd them by a force
> Above the power of deaths divorce
> One flame of love thir lives did bvrne
> Even to ashes in their vrne
> They dy, but not depart, who meet
> In wedding and in winding sheet
> Whom God hath knit so firm in one
> Admit no separacion
> Therefore vnto one marble trist
> Wee leave there now vnited dvst
> As roote in earth embrace to rise
> Most lovely flowers in paradise

Two more unique features of Haccombe Church are the freestone carved sleeved or vested arms that project, one from the chancel wall and the other, damaged, from the west aisle. The undamaged arm ends in a large clasped hand which is perforated, and was probably intended to hold a torch or candle that burned before – or above – the effigy of a saint, or could perhaps have held a banner stave.

Among the early stained-glass windows are several small panels of Flemish painted glass said to have been taken from the medieval Haccombe House. They are similar in style, although cruder, to the exquisite small panels depicting charming scenes of secular and domestic life as well as sacred subjects in the Upper Reading Room of the Bodleian Library, Oxford, which date from the sixteenth and seventeeth centuries, and which in many cases have also come from houses.

The beautiful medieval encaustic tiles on the church floor include twenty-seven different designs. Most are local made, but a few blue ones may have been brought back by pilgrims to Santiago di Compostella.

There is one more unusual detail at Haccombe. One whole, and one half, horseshoe are nailed to the outside of the old south door. They are supposed to record the wager made between a Carew of Haccombe, and a Champernowne of Dartington, on who could swim his horse furthest\into the sea at Torquay. A nineteenth-century ballad written long after the event records the contest, won by Carew, who rode home to Haccombe and nailed his horse's shoes to the church door, proving his ownership. But there are traces of two other shoes on the door which show the four to have been placed in the form of a cross. This was an old charm against witches, so possibly superstition inspired the ballad.

Haccombe does not feel haunted despite its age and remoteness and the well-stocked charnel house in the crypt. Its warm stones seem to offer peace and hope, as it stands in its valley as rooted as the background of tall ancient ilexes.

Two source-streams rise to become the oak-shawled river that shares its name with the moor. East Dart Head is south of Cranmere and West Dart rises east of Mis Tor. The east branch is the wilder of the two in its moorland course, with waterfalls and a rushing mood, the West Dart is tamed by the cutting out of it of the Devonport Leat above Wistman's Wood. By the time they come together at Dartmeet they are both powerfully mature, their channels studded with giant granite boulders smoothed by the waters' force, in places so close together that they form stepping stones, exciting alternatives to the new road and old clapper bridge. The rivers have rolled the moorstone rocks down from the heights in their winter rages and the impatient water coursing among them produces the weird "cry", and its attendant stories and legends of sinister magical attraction that lures the unwary to death by drowning in the clutches of this strong brown god.

Like the moor itself, the Devon rivers demand respect, particularly in winter; in summer one can wade in places among the boulders and sometimes be surprised by the cool, evanescent touch of a trout or even salmon against one's legs; or follow the Dart where there are public paths, past New Bridge and Holne Bridge, down to Buckfastleigh, and on past another medieval bridge at Staverton to Dartington, where it curves broad and calm for the first time before it reaches Totnes and then, below the weir, becomes tidal and navigable. Cargoes of Scandinavian timber are still unloaded at the old quays, and pleasure boats ply between Totnes and Dartmouth.

For the first couple of miles of the twelve to Dartmouth the river runs as straight as a canal, bounded by colourful, hilly, arable land at the very heart of the South Hams. In October the shining crimson flesh of new plough, echoed by the beeches in the woods, alternates with the delicate green of winter wheat already a few inches high. Winter seems foreign to the valleys that run to the river; two western ones that carry the tributary streams of Harbourne and Wash make spring feel the normal intensely growing state of nature. After the straight stretch two peninsulas to the east and west force the river to make a sharp "S" bend. On top of the steep and graciously wooded western promontory is Sharpham House, built in 1805 on an older site with sweeping Capability Brown grounds and an idyllic boathouse far below at the waterside. To hear baroque music at Sharpham in the oval first-floor music room whose windows view the deepening violet summer evening sky above the plunging lines of the trees, with the moon's lamp brightening with each moment and purple shadows in the river valley, is a rare delight.

Above an inlet on the east bank a mile or so further down river is the village of Stoke Gabriel. Its church is in some danger of being usurped by the biggest yew-tree in the county, a vast edifice of a tree almost as high as the church tower, whose dull red branches curve to the ground and run along it, to embrace tombstones and lean anciently on stout forked sticks. To stand near the great bole of it feels like being in a huge dark-green tent; it is eerie yet not repellent. Some claim that the tree is 1500 years old. The church has a thirteenth-century west tower, the rest is fifteenth-century. It contains an unusual monument to the memory of "Tamosin, wife of Mr Peter Lyde, who died 25 February 1663". It is on the chancel wall, carved in limestone in typical endearingly *naïf* manner, black-painted and surrounded with sprays of natural stone-coloured laurel. On the heart is engraved:

> Long may thy name as long as marble last
> Beloved Tamosin thovgh vnder clods her cast.
> This formal heart doth trvly signify
> Twixt wife and hvsband cordiell vnity
> If to be graccivs doth reqvire dve praise
> Let Tamosin have it she deservs ye bayes.

Above the heart is carved a flame.

Opposite Stoke Gabriel at the top of a long inlet, Bow Creek, is picturesque Tuckenhay, once a considerable little port handling cargoes of road-stone, and where two paper mills and a cornmill made it a busy nineteenth-century place. One paper-mill worked until the 1960s, and the buildings are now transformed into pleasant holiday apartments.

On the east side of the river again, a mile past Stoke Gabriel, Sandridge House lies on a hill overlooking the river with a view rivalling Sharpham's. This Italianate house from the same date, 1805, occupies the site of an earlier mansion. John Davis, the Elizabethan navigator, was probably born at Sandridge Barton nearby. A couple of miles away, above the mile-wide stretch of river between Dittisham and Galmpton Creek with its heronry, Adrian, John and Humphrey Gilbert had their childhood home at Greenway, where Agatha Christie's modern house looks over to Dittisham with its plum orchards and Ferry Inn. From here onwards the river becomes the busy harbour and port of Dartmouth, the bird-haunted, peaceful reaches give way to the felt proximity of the sea beyond the castle-guarded, still wooded mouth of this history-laden river.

The Devonshire Avon rises north-west of Peter's Boundstone, on Ryder's Hill above Huntingdon Warren, and flows twenty-two miles to the sea. The young river passes between the remains of tinners' huts and is spanned by a clapper bridge near Huntingdon

Cross on the Abbot's Way. Soon it runs into the Avon Dam Reservoir; there is no public road anywhere near this long stretch of water, whose upper end away from the huge concrete dam seems always to have existed, wild yet serene as the rest of the moor. Below the dam a tarred track follows the river, fringed by rowans bright with scarlet berries in late summer, down to its first bridge at Shipley hamlet. After this it runs through South Brent where it powered the mills, and under the motor road A38. From here to its mouth this particularly clear and diamonded river, that still accommodates a few salmon and quite plentiful trout and eel, traverses some of the most peaceful and lovely reaches of the South Hams. The villages of Avon Wick and Diptford are surrounded by ancient farmhouses in their secluded combes, homes that have held the lives of families for centuries in their mellow, sheltering walls: this sense of continuity that has survived in South Devon is a prime reason for the pull of the place, its human genius blending with the far more ancient landscape. It is an almost perfect distribution of settlements, each having privacy yet placed within easy reach of others.

The banks are wooded now for most of the way, and although lanes accompany the river in some stretches, the course of the old railway in the valley is overgrown with alder and hazel scrub, and the water meadows are tranquil. The valley is deep in places and the approaches to the several bridges wind down precipitously. Along the riverside path from Gara Bridge, once a station, whose buildings are now privately owned, are several pairs of imposing gateposts belonging to the Victorian Hazelwood estate, with old rhododendrons on a small island, and trees overhanging a calm straight stretch where the water is mysterious and Lethean, yet still remembering days when boating parties launched from the Gothic, two-storeyed boathouse now falling into ruin, with a few climbing roses clinging to its crumbling sides. In August the river-banks here are guarded by ranks and groups of the tall, pea-flowered Himalayan Balsam whose sweet flowers range in colour from white to pink to purple. Mosses and lichens clothe the oaks where the path is high and slippery above the river before picturesque Topsham Bridge.

A little further along are two old mills that ground flour for the hilltop village of Loddiswell perched on the steep western side.

Shortly after this the river takes a sharp curve westward and meanders through the marshy reaches of its once much larger estuary to the long bridge at Aveton Gifford, where the present four-mile-long tidal reach begins. A tidal road leads from Aveton Gifford to Ringmore and Bigbury, covered at high tide and always a pleasure tinged with excitement to drive along. It is called The Sticks from the poles that mark out the hard road from the mud on either side where it crosses inlets; one of these is swathed with a grey-pink mist of sea-asters in August. The quagmire is at least four feet deep, densely populated with worms and hence birds: gulls and terns in variety, oystercatchers sleek in black and white, red-hosed, piping their haunting cry, trios of even more chic little ringed plovers, turnstones, dunlins, and further down-river the fishing herons spaced out one-legged at their solemn stations. The small oaks that grow to the water's edge here as along the Dart have had their lower branches clipped as if a giant with a pair of shears had been at work.

About halfway to the sea the mud gives way to golden sand, firm to walk on, a wide expanse on each side of the shallow river at low tide. At the curved mouth, before the sand bar whose breakers play tricks on unwary boats entering the estuary to moor half a mile from the sea at Bantham anchorage, Bantham Ham is a variation on the sandspits of Dawlish Warren and Teignmouth. It consists of raised dunes covered partly with marram grass, on low cliffs of Devonian rock, here a narrow section of Wembury Siltstones, with a small spit of sand uncovered at low water. The tidal current's boisterous meeting with the Avon's waters creates a fierce sweep in and out of the idyllic harbour.

Erme Head emerges from the blanket bog north of the prehistoric Erme Pound, which lies to the south of Cater's Beam, only one and a half miles from Plym Head. The stream of the Erme runs briskly by the extensive ancient sites, keeping pace with a stone row, crosses Erme Plains, and after about five miles skirts the dwarf oak copse of Higher Piles below Harford Moor. In spring after snows the ground about this solitudinous area is littered with sheep skulls and bones that with the rows, circles and loose patterns of clitter form what reads like a cryptic message. After another mile, the river cuts deeper and deeper into its valley as the moor ends, with

Harford moorgate above on the east side; below it, medieval Harford Bridge spans the Erme. Harford consists of a farm, a few houses and the little sixteenth-century moorland granite church with brasses commemorating Thomas Williams (1513–1566), Speaker to the House of Commons, and John Prideaux, both of neighbouring Stowford.

A lane leads down on the east side of the river to Ivybridge, but it is possible to walk down along the west bank, through rough but beautiful woodland. It is particularly fine in spring when the Erme is in full flood, running through steep, densely wooded Stowford Cleave; here the river is quite wide in places, with torrents and waterfalls rushing and cascading among the rocks. Stowford Lodge, high above the east bank, is a Domesday manor with a long history, now a conference centre for the Royal Agricultural Society of England. A little below this is Stowford Paper Mill. In 1787 William Dunsterville, a Plymouth miller, bought Stowford Barton and built on the land the large paper mill that is still operating today. The water of the Erme is pure and soft and needs less treatment than hard water to prepare for papermaking; a million gallons of it are used daily. Other paper mills were built further down the river, but Stowford Mill survives as an example of the gracious industrial architecture of the eighteenth century. On one of his visits to Devon, J. V. Turner made several sketches of the buildings, beloved by the mill's historian, Mr B. R. Northmoor, whose family have worked at the mill for generations.

At the end of its descent from the moor the Erme rushes down into Ivybridge. The modern town begins now immediately below Stowford, but in Thomas Westcote's day there was no settlement of note around the bridge itself, which he described: "Here he [Erme] is crowned with a bridge named Ivy which that it takes denomination of that creeping tapestry wherewith it is totally covered, I cannot aver, but it is very probable." The early clapper bridge was probably built to convey traffic going upcountry from Plymouth in the thirteenth century, and for the convenience of farmers, tinners and millers. It was recorded as Ponte Ederoso in 1250 and Ivybrugge in 1292, and is sited at the junction where four ancient parishes met: the large parish of Cornwood, and Harford, Ugborough and Ermington, all with fine churches. No church was built at Ivybridge, where a village slowly grew up, until 1789.

In 1848 Isambard Kingdom Brunel's famous South Devon Railway, later the Great Western, reached Ivybridge, and the viaduct across the Erme valley, constructed of stone and timber, was a magnificent achievement. Ivybridge Station was in use until 1959, and there are moves now to reopen it. Some of the pillars that supported Brunel's creation, replaced in 1893 by a stone viaduct, remain, romantically draped in ivy, and from beneath them you can see Stowford Lodge high up on the other side of the cleave.

One of the Victorian residents of Ivybridge who must have welcomed the railway's advent was William Cotton, who lived at Highlands, a large house a little way up the Cornwood road, hidden in dense shrubberies. The best view of it, and the whole of Ivybridge, is from the top of Westlake Hill, reached from the new bridge over the A38.

The original Highlands was built in 1790; William Cotton acquired it in 1839, probably encouraged to move to Devon by his friend Sir Joshua Reynolds of nearby Plympton. Cotton enlarged Highlands to accommodate his unique collection of early prints, drawings and bronzes, now in Plymouth Art Gallery. The rooms at Highlands are lofty and well-lit, and from the tower there are wide views over the Erme Valley. The grounds are filled with an immense variety of ornamental trees, a small arboretum in itself, and flowering shrubs such as rhododendron and azaleas, magnolia, camellia, tree ferns and much more.

After William Cotton's death in 1865 the property saw various changes of ownership. It was bought in 1977 by Sergeant T. L. Lucas and his wife Molly, who are enthusiastically restoring it. The house has experienced the sort of change that happens to many large properties in this century, in this case divided into three separate dwellings, and the grounds split up as well.

Ivybridge is an interesting example of the growth of a new town. Its Urban District Council was formed in 1894 and functioned until 1935 when it was absorbed by Plympton St Mary UDC and Ivybridge reduced to a parish. Then on 17 June 1977 it was given the status of a town with a town council and mayor. The site had been chosen for expansion in the 1950s, and the history of the development is a story of plans and counter-plans, objections and decisions, delays and changes. The population will expand from the 1962 figure of 1775 to perhaps 11,000. Now Ivybridge has almost all the amenities and appurtenances of a complete town, although it is not yet self-supporting as regards employment. Its cheerful, largely young community presents a heart-warming contrast to decay and inner-city problems. From Westlake Hill one can meditate on the visible sweep of history from Bronze Age settlement through medieval and Victorian ways of life to our opportunity- and problem-filled twentieth-century world.

After Ivybridge the Erme winds quietly through a generous valley for two miles to Ermington, with its open square above the church which has a slightly leaning spire. The village is a Domesday settlement, around it a necklace of Saxon and Celtic farms and earlier mansions. The interior of the mainly fourteenth-century church is joyously animated with wood carvings in every available surface, giving the impression of a forest filled with living creatures and vegetation, so vitally, warmly and humorously represented that the animals – deer, squirrels, monkeys, rabbits, snakes, birds, small rodents – seem poised for instant flight, or are, like some of the owls, actually in flight, with spread wings. The carving is the work of Violet Pinwill and her six sisters, daughters of the rector from 1880, Edmund Pinwill. Violet became a much-sought-after artist and teacher with a Plymouth workshop employing a number of craftsmen, whose work appears in churches all over Devon and Cornwall and elsewhere.

The tree-lined river has another two miles to run before reaching its tidal estuary. It passes several fine houses, in settings well-chosen by Saxon and Norman landowners in this classically beautiful and sheltered park-like area. The largest is Flete on the west bank off the Modbury–Plymouth road that crosses the Erme at Sequers Bridge. Fleet estate covers both banks of the Erme and included several other large houses. Flete itself, whose nineteenth-century camelot towers can be seen through the trees from the main road, was Saxon, Norman, Tudor and Victorian by turn, owned by great families like the Heles and Bulteels. In the mid-nineteenth century John Bulteel's fortunes declined and with his wife Euphemia, so beautiful she was known as "Moonbeam", he moved to Pamflete, a delightfully situated old farmhouse, once a mansion, further down the Erme. Flete became the residence of Lord Mildmay, and the neighbouring estate of Membland the home of Lord Revelstoke.

Flete is an enormous house, last substantially enlarged by the Victorian architect Norman Shaw from 1878 onwards. It is now divided into forty apartments for retired people, self-owned, whose only obligation is to manage the gardens: a big under-taking, which they have achieved successfully, bringing the grounds with their shrub-lined borders and glorious trees back to much of their former glory.

Through the Erme's embracing woodlands that form part of the Flete estate wind romantic nineteenth-century carriage drives. Many of the landowners of the period gave their employees winter work constructing these rides for their own and their guests' pleasure. To judge from the traditions, Queen Victoria spent much time being driven through Devonshire woods! Lord Membland made the nine-mile drive from his house near Noss Mayo, it runs for several miles in a spectacularly scenic route along the cliffs east of Stoke Point before turning inland to circle back to the house. The Duke of Bedford made a five-mile drive from his *cottage orné* at Endsleigh on the Tamar to the river port of Morwellham. Many others, long and short, are marked on maps. All, where open to the public, make wonderful walks.

The Erme estuary is like the Avon in its base of firm golden sand, and its bird and fish colonies. The deeper woodlands furnish it with additional beauty and mystery, and there can be a wildness at the mouth, which, Leland wrote, "is no haven, but periculous rokkes", although it is shallow enough to ford at low tide; a friend of mine tells the story of how she caught a ten-pound salmon with her two small hands as it tried to escape through the shallows, and gave a poached dinner-party for ten with it.

The Yealm rises two miles south of Erme Head. It soon slips down the side of a rise thickly covered with clitter, then past evi-dence of tin streaming, and in one and a half miles from its source enters the high valley woodland called Hawns and Dendles. We camped for a night in Hawns one August night of full moon, and, having asked permission at Higher Hele, we pitched our tent beside the young river in a perfectly circular glade of sessile oaks. Further up the hillside the deciduous trees are caped by a conifer plantation; there are several hut circles in these woods, and some of the paths through them are emerald grassy rides,

more carriage drives, made by the Rogers family of Blachford
Park, Cornwood.

We were fortunate in choosing a night of ideal weather. The
woods were too welcoming and brightly lit for any of the grimmer
aspects of the moor to be apparent, and the only discomfort we
experienced was a savage attack at dusk by midges. But as the moon
rose they vanished as quickly as they had massed. Next morning was
perfect as well; chaffinches and robins sang to the accompaniment of
the river's quiet murmur, and a dragonfly alighted on my arm. After
breakfast I watched a small brown trout in one of the river pools, and
as we were walking up to the moor a pair of young buzzards wheeled
and mewed above us. That day we met only three other persons, a
walker heading for Yealm Head, with its Bronze Age settlement,
and two shepherds with dogs and binoculars. The open moor
presented its loveliest face, with the sun beating down on the
aromatic heath, distant ponies grazing and the lightest of breezes.

About a mile south of the woods the Yealm comes to the village
of Cornwood, where it is dammed into a lake in the grounds of
Blachford Park. The parish contains many interesting houses,
including Hanger Farm, Great and Little Stert, Slade and Blachford, all chosen for their sheltered sites below the moor and out of
the prevailing winds. Perhaps the most important of them historically is Fardel Manor, between Cornwood and Ivybridge, a
meticulously preserved and restored medieval mansion, although
on a smaller scale than Dartington.

The great dining-hall on the ground floor, reached through the
present drawing-room with its huge fireplace, was divided until
recently by an upper storey which was removed to reveal the
barrel-vaulted ceiling. The stone mullioned windows have retained
their original fastenings for the shutters that were used in lieu of
glass and iron bars. The original massive oak doors and colossal
lock and key-holes are there still, and some of the oak screen in the
drawing-room.

On the first floor is a room with an early English window and a
window seat, which was most likely the ladies' solar. A door from
the housekeeper's room, with one small, high window, gave access
to rooms over the great hall, now removed, where at night
Victorian housekeepers would lock the menservants into the
furthest room and the womenservants into the the next one.

The present owners have carried out thorough repairs to both the interior and exterior of the house. Some of the ancient hung slates on the outer wall of the oldest section, and the newer seventeenth-century ones on the wall having a sixteenth-century porch adorned with stone figures of a rampant lion and leopard, were replaced with new slates brought from Cumbria where the slates quarried today match the colour of the originals. They are blue with a brownish tinge, melting into the surrounding landscape colours.

Fardel is sited on a prehistoric trackway between the rivers Erme and Plym. In the past there were standing stones nearby, and here was found the first stone with an Ogham inscription to be discovered in England. The Fardel stone is now in the British Museum. The buildings stand on a granite outcrop of Dartmoor that raised the site above the surrounding valley that would have been marshy when the house was built.

The restoration of an ancient house is an act of faith that keeps us in touch with the past. It is concerned not only with the conservation of stones and wood that have been selected, cut, dressed and built into an architectural form, but also to emphasize that a historic house provides more than a setting for birth, love, work and death. It enriches the quality of life with its atmosphere and continuity. Fardel is not open to the general public, but the owners believe that such historic homes should be places that people are aware of and can share in various ways.

For much of its southward course the Yealm flows parallel with the Erme at only two or three miles' distance. Past Yealmpton on the west, the Kitley estate occupies a peninsula formed by the Yealm and the little river Silverbridge. Kitley was the Tudor home of the Pollexfens and then the Bastards of Gerston near Kingsbridge. The rockbase here is limestone, once quarried in the park as Kitley marble, with a green tinge. Further east it is pink. In both quarrying areas are caves, those at Kitley contain some beautiful stalactite and stalagmite formations despite damage; it is a strange place, surrounded by immensely tall alders and birches, dripping mosses on the steep old quarry sides.

On the Yealm's east bank nearby is Puslinch, a rosy Queen Anne-style house built in 1718 by James Yonge, a naval surgeon whose niece was Charlotte Yonge the sentimental novelist. Here the estuary begins, joined after a mile by that of the Cofflete Creek; the tidal waters cover fourteen miles, and are met at Newton Ferrers by another creek running west–east to Bridge End and Noss Mayo. The swift current swirls up and down the Y-shaped estuary arms and round the promontory of Warren Point to lead in another mile to the sea. There is a profusion of marine flora and fauna in this estuary, including cockle beds and cultivated oysters, and great shoals of grey mullet move shadowily under the moored boats' hulls in this perfect anchorage.

An enormous variety of trees throng the banks as densely as those of the Erme valley. The tough, hardy native oak predominates, accompanied by ash, fine beeches, sweet chestnut, the ubiquitous sycamore and some birch and wild cherry. Landowners' plantings of evergreens have here been judiciously placed among the broad-leaved trees and the darker colours of pine and Douglas Fir add, with the sunny springtime plumage of larch, strength to the shading of colours. On the floor of these creekside woods, springtime spreads pink and white coverings of anemones after the celandines' glossy gold, huge pink-stemmed primroses border the rides before the bluebells' blaze and sweet scent. Later in open glades there are drifts of pink-violet rose bay willow herb and beneath it the dusty yellow of cow-wheat and the bright gold of tormentil. The woods and the estuary are the habitat of over 150 species of birds, day-fliers, night-fliers and seabirds, many gulls, shags, cormorants; occasionally a gannet, that diver *par excellence*, comes in from the sea. Numerous duck species come here, including families of exotic black and white clad shelduck with a brown scarf around back and chest, red bill and pink legs. There are resident birds of prey such as buzzards, kestrels and sparrow-hawks, and occasional visits from peregrines, merlins, hobbys and ospreys. Ravens, solitary or in pairs, announce themselves with sepulchral croak, and the busy communities of rookeries, such a cheerful part of the rural scene, have moved to new tree colonies since the elms' demise. With the exception of the golden eagle and a few others, most English birds can be seen in the Yealm estuary. At night all the creatures of witchcraft are abroad: owls, at least six species of bat, snakes and toads; and foxes, badgers and otters are shyer denizens.

The river that gives the city of Plymouth its name rises at Plym Head

just north of Duck Pool and south of Crane Hill, a mile to the
north of Erme Head. The Plym flows south-west, south of
Hartor, entering the moorland valley called Drizzlecombe with its
concentration of prehistorical monuments, hut groups, cists, and a
sanctuary comprising stone rows and three standing stones, one
almost eighteen feet in height. Not especially tall seen from a
distance, the menhir grows as you approach it and its strange power
is felt, enigmatic, yet despite its mystery communicating an
extraordinary aura, even more impressive than if it bore
Ogham script or Roman inscription. At the end of the sanctuary
beneath Eastern Tor is Ditsworthy Warren House, once the home
of the warrener who managed the rabbits up on Ditsworthy
Warren a mile to the north. It is a bleak enough granite house in a
walled enclosure, but modernized as an excursion centre.

Steadily descending, the river comes in three miles to Cadover
Bridge, an ancient crossing where the flat banks now make it a
favourite picnic place for Plymothians. Two miles on again is the
Plym's confluence with the Meavy, the gull-river. Above the
rivers' meeting place on Dewer Stone Hill the name of the
Dartmoor poet N. T. Carrington is cut upon a rock. From here
onwards the Plym runs through Bickleigh Vale and Plym Forest,
an extensive woodland partly owned by the National Trust. The
nineteenth-century historical painter Benjamin Haydon, whose
great unsaleable canvases reflect his own stormy life ended in
suicide, spent much time in this beautiful valley in whose shadowy
depths he found inspiration. But in a few miles more the Plym
enters the environs of Plymouth, reaches its tidal estuary at
Crabtree opposite Saltram House and flows under Laira road bridge
before becoming the Cattewater with docks in its inlets on both
sides, Oreston on the east and ancient Sutton Pool, with the trawler
harbour, on the west. At Mount Batten Point opposite the Citadel
it merges with The Sound.

The Meavy, although flowing into the Plym, is a river to be
reckoned with in its own right. It rises south of Princetown, and
after a couple of miles enters the woods surrounding Burrator
Reservoir, filled with its dammed-up waters. Emerging from the
dam in a mile, it takes a turn to the west. Here it fills a little valley
with its song, as it rushes past the hill where a thirteenth-century

waymark, Marchants Cross, stands, and on below the village bearing its name. Meavy has a partly Norman church, near it the Meavy oak that is claimed to be of the same age, huge if battered, on the green where is also the Inn, a famed place for locals and walkers to foregather. Soon after this the Meavy, grown in size and now a swift torrent, turns southward to canter past Hoo Meavy and Goodameavy villages to its meeting with the Plym.

The source of the Tavy is south of Cut Hill half a mile west of Dart Head, yet another unfailing source welling out of the great peat placenta. It winds north-west at first, to join the Amicombe Brook, itself previously augmented by the Black Ridge Brook, and in another mile or two by the Rattle Brook: a felicitous name for such a brisk stream. So that the Tavy is already a considerable force now as it enters Tavy Cleave, one of the deepest and wildest gorges of the High Moor with "stationary blasts of waterfalls" rivalling those of Lustleigh Cleave and Becka Falls, if not as spectacular as the White Lady in Lydford Gorge. Tavy Cleave is unique for the enormous amount of clitter on its steep sides, resembling the results of a berserk giant's vandalization of the rocks. The cataracts fall over great square and oblong chunks of granite broken from the tors' weathered cracks. The sight stays in the mind long after legs have stopped aching from the effort of scrambling among the boulders, and the insistent clamour of the Tavy's voice has faded.

A few miles further on the river is bridged for the first time at Hill Bridge and puts on a collar of trees as it descends from the moor midway between the moorland parishes of Mary Tavy and Peter Tavy. Then it continues to the beautiful town of Tavistock, elegant with buildings of Green Hurdwick stone, many built by the Duke of Bedford in the great nineteenth-century mining era, its abbey ruins and busy modern life.

In 1803 an amazing engineering feat was begun when the Tavistock canal was taken from the river in the centre of the town to run four miles to Morwellham Quay on the Tamar; it was found necessary to construct a two-mile-long tunnel in the middle to take the canal underneath Morwell Down, and the tunnellers, working from each side of the hill, met exactly in the middle. The work, designed by John Taylor and largely carried out by French prisoners of war, was completed by 1817 and the canal was used to transport ore from the mines to Tavistock by men "footing" long barges: lying down in them and "walking" along the tunnel roof.

Below Tavistock the river soon enters richly sheltering woods for the rest of its serpentine journey to the estuary. About four miles from Tavistock it is joined at Double Waters by the River Walkham, that itself rises one mile south-west of Tavy Head. The two rivers make a powerfully sweeping force; at Denham Bridge, not far from Drake's home, Buckland Abbey, there is a warning notice announcing that the water is forty feet deep between the confining ten-foot gap between its rocky sides. In some ways it is like a smaller version of the the Brig o' Dee – and yet there is every difference. The Tavy, noble and proud though it is, is in every way a Devonshire river, often lulled to peace by the warm beneficence of the landscape, while the Dee's majestic proportions and highland ancestry are altogether more daunting. Near the ancient house of Marystow on the east bank the Tavy estuary begins, to meet the Tamar three miles further along on the outskirts of Plymouth.

The Tamar, the last river of South Devon, begins its sixty-mile journey just across the Cornish border at Woolley Barrows half a mile east of the A39, in an area of carboniferous shales and sandstones. It flows through arable country, augmented by several sizeable tributaries, the Rivers Ottery, Carey, Kensey, Wolf, Thrushel and Lyd, then in another thirty miles meets the Inny below Bishop's Rock in the green fastnesses of Dunterue Wood where it forms a huge "U". In another thirty miles, its curves now generous, it comes to Blanchdown Wood, and is in mining country. At the edges of Dartmoor here the weathering of the granite allowed the formation of tin, copper, lead, iron, wolfram, silver and arsenic. From Gunnislake, where Gunnislake Rock, or Chimney Rock, stands up like an archetypal mining symbol in granite, signs of the industry remain: memorial chimneys bravely thrusting out of the woods towards the sky, old workings and heaps, all now abandoned. On the far side of another great turn is the once-busy port of Morwellham, where the ore rush from the Duke of Bedford's mines was handled.

About 1844 copper was discovered on the Duke's land at Blanchdown. The Devon Great Consols Mine was opened, and by the mid-1850s it and others at Morwellham were some of the most productive mines in the world. Shares bought at £1 rocketed to £200. But by the end of the century the boom was over; however, during the fifty years of its life a complex system of extraction and transport had been evolved. The Tamar was navigable as far as Morwellham and ships had been bringing lime up to it from Plymouth for burning in the kilns that still stand beside the quay, to be used on the fields above the steep wooded valley sides. New huge quays were built for the three-masters that took away the ore. It was transported to the quays by trucks running along a network of railways. The most ambitious of these was the inclined plane railway leading from the end of the Tavistock Canal at the top of the eastern valley-side above the quays. The trucks ran downhill and were pushed the last stretch to the docks.

The reopening of the abandoned river port as a recreation and research centre seventy years on is an enterprise for the Dartington Amenities Research Trust, who run the scheme, to be proud of. Volunteers slaved to remove silt and rubbish from the quays and an immense amount has been achieved in thirteen years. There are museums, marked trails, dray rides along the Duke's drive to Endsleigh, and a tramway trip into the reopened George and Charlotte Mine. The Great Dock, the raised railway, the manganese barn, assayer's laboratory, blacksmith's and cooper's shops have been restored. There are plans to make more use of the river again and possibly to start more mining.

The sides of the densely-wooded gorge through which the Tamar runs at Morwellham are scattered with granite outcrops whose fissures gave openings to the ore lodes. Where the quays were built there is a wider riverside area, and this is the pattern along these lower reaches: high cliffs on one side with a sheltered river valley bottom on the other; the silt accumulated on these flatter areas make them marvellously fertile and the strawberries and tomatoes grown in the drowned valley are richly-coloured and luscious.

Tamar is an imposing river from here onwards, forming another enormous peninsula before dropping down to meet the Tavy estuary, then the St Germans, that stretches far into Cornwall, before changing its name to Hamoaze where it narrows between Devonport and Torpoint and is naval mooring ground, where the great grey ships lie demonstrating tight-lipped maritime history. Now the Tamar moves majestically on its tides, past St John's Lake and Millbrook Lake, and through the last narrows at Devil's Point into The Sound.

Chapter Six

BUCKFASTLEIGH AND SOUTH BRENT

THE PARISH CHURCH of Buckfastleigh, part thirteenth-, part fifteenth-century, stands high upon the limestone cliff that provides the surrounding quarries with their material. From it there is a wide view over Dartmoor and the Dart Valley. It is hard to believe that this hill was once under water during an interglacial period one million years ago. There are the ruins of a chantry chapel in the churchyard which, says Sabine Baring-Gould, had a pardoner's room above it. In front of the south porch is the heavily enclosed tomb of Richard Cabell of Brook Manor, a fine house about a mile to the north-west on the skirts of the moor beside the little Mardle River. In Sabine Baring-Gould's *Devon* we read that he was the sort of squireen, "the last male of his race", who acquired a Bluebeard type of reputation and was doubtless a seducer of village maidens. The legend arose that after his death in 1677, "fiends and black dogs breathing fire raced over Dartmoor and surrounded Brook, howling". It may well be that some small children are still told not to put fingers through the chinks in Sir Richard's tomb or he will grab them and drag them inside. But on a sunny spring day the churchyard is an attractive place with many graves trimly adorned with sparkling pink granite chips and fine headstones. I went into the church and found the great Bible open at the perfect place for such a day of life rather than death: The Song of Solomon.

However, the church does not stand upon firm foundations, or at least, not the solid ones you might expect. Underneath it is a splendid honeycomb of limestone caves, not yet by any means fully explored. Although early travellers like Dean Jeremiah Milles and Polwhele recorded the interest and beauty of the area and saw the quarries that had existed for centuries before their own, the eighteenth, they did not discover the extent of the caves. The earliest explorer to realize their importance was the Rev. J. MacEnery in the 1820s. He was followed by William Pengelly. (Both these men carried out the early explorations at Kent's

Cavern, Torquay.) Pengelly wrote of the Buckfastleigh caves in the mid-nineteenth century: "I have sometimes thought that Buckfastleigh might appropriately be called the Metropolis of Devonshire Caverns, so numerous do they seem to be in the locality."

The caves were formed by water draining away through the porous limestone in successive phases of heat and cold. But little more serious study of the caves was done, although much scrambling that caused damage, until 1939, when the five caves in Higher Kiln Quarry were properly investigated, and two important discoveries made: extensions to Reed's Cave and, most exciting of all, the bone deposit in Joint Mitnor Cave. In two years over 4000 bones and teeth from animals living in the final warm interglacial period of the Ice Age were dug up. They were found in a conical mass inside the cave, and included bones of bison, elephant, hippo, rhino, lion, hyaena, wolf, and red, giant and fallow deer. England at one stage had a climate like that of Africa today. How was this amazing ossuary composed? It appears that through the action of successive hot and cold phases in which the caves were formed there was also cracking of the earth's surface, and a hole was created, probably covered by underbrush, through which unsuspecting animals fell down into the cave and were trapped. Smaller marauders like hyaenas may even have jumped down into it attracted by the smell of decaying carcasses, and been trapped in their turn. So the cone of bone grew, until later the hole was again closed by earth movement, protected and partially grown over with stalagmites. Now this cave has been so excavated that visitors (by appointment at the cave centre nearby) can walk in and look at the section of the cone that has been only partially excavated in order to show the layers of bones *in situ*. This provides another of Devon's dizzying flashback-in-time experiences. There are a number of other limestone caves in the region, a similar animal trap at Eastern Torrs Quarry, Yealmpton, near the Kitley Caves with their beautiful stalagmites, open to the public, Windmill Cave at Brixham, that contained flint tools as well as bones of mammoth and lion, but is not open, the caves and fine rock outcrops at Chudleigh, and a very deep cave at Torbryan. Best known of all is Kent's Cavern, Torquay. Here, in addition to the flint implements proving the presence of palaeolithic man in Devon, were found similar animal bones to those at Buckfastleigh, and also bones from

Wooden dredger, built c. 1900, in the Teign Estuary

Torquay

Dartmouth, the Buttermarket

Berry Head, near Brixham

Old Brixham and New

Dartmouth towards Kingswear

Torcross and Slapton Sands

the mammoth, cave and grizzly bear, bison, sabre-toothed tiger, reindeer, Irish elk and horse. Many of the cave finds are housed in Torquay Natural History Museum. At Buckfastleigh is the first Cave Studies Centre to be established in Britain, named after William Pengelly. It also runs a small museum, which, with a lecture room, has been constructed in old farm buildings at Higher Kiln Quarry. Two of the other caves at Higher Kiln are conserved for special reasons: Rift Cave for the study of the colony of bats who live in it, protected from vandals by old iron bedsteads attached to the rock! Reed's Cave has particularly fine formations; it leads into a maze of caverns and tunnels that is used for cave exploration training that can involve a two-hour crawl. There is another cave at Pridhamsleigh Quarry on the east side of the main road on the Exeter side of Buckfastleigh, also used for caving. The Dart handily runs nearby to accommodate cavers wishing to rid themselves of the layers of mud they acquire underground. A friend who takes schoolchildren caving once got into trouble with irate mums who objected to their girls stripping off to bra and pants and plunging into the Dart, to the delight of passing lorry drivers.

Just to the north of Buckfastleigh is the original settlement of Buckfast beside the Dart, where now the great establishment of Buckfast Abbey draws pilgrims and tourists in thousands. It has a breathtakingly long life story with a happy ending. Founded in 1018 by Duke Aethelwerd, it was endowed by King Knut, that good, firm Danish Christian king. The Benedictine foundation suffered vicissitudes, became Cistercian and then again Benedictine. With other religious houses it was suppressed at the Dissolution, in 1539, and by 1796 the great building was a sad ruin. In 1806 a private house was built out of the stones, which still stands; then in 1882 a community of displaced French Benedictines bought the property. With help from the Lord Clifford of the day, other benefactors, and mostly themselves, the monks began to rebuild the Abbey in 1907. By 1922 they were able to open the church for public worship, and by 1938 the entire building plan had been realized.

The inspired determination of the monks, from the young abbot Anscar Vonier, who was aged thirty in 1882 and who made the rebuilding of Buckfast Abbey his life's work, to Brother Peter, the mason, who passed every single stone that went to make the resurrected abbey through his hands to the builders, never faltered. Abbot Vonier died a few weeks after the final stone was put in place, in 1938, Brother Peter a few years ago at the age of ninety-three. The Benedictine motto, *Ora et labora* must have had countless unseen results as well as the architectural showpiece we see today, and it has been further adorned in more recent years through the artistic creations of various people, perhaps most notably by Dom Charles Norris, the stained-glass artist. He went to Buckfast as a young man about 1930 and began to work with stained glass after two or three years, when he was studying at the Royal College of Art. In addition to taking his share in the later stages of the building work he was in the Army with General Montgomery in Africa during World War Two. Then his reputation as a glassmaker began to grow until now he is far too busy to undertake every stage of the work for a commission himself, and has two other monks working as full-time assistants in his workshop. Dom Charles does the designing and makes the aluminium sections into which the pieces of glass are fitted. To date, the team has made windows for 130 churches, including several in Plymouth.

Dom Charles's great contribution to Buckfast Abbey is the huge east window with the figure of Christ standing with welcoming arms outstretched behind an altar table, in the modern chapel built as an addition to the main Abbey church as a place for quiet prayer, especially used during the summer when thousands of visitors form part of the life of Buckfast. The entire wall from floor to ceiling, apart from the cross supports, is glass, in many colours, but, or so is the impression I always take away, in predominant blues and greens of the most glorious shades, as if the essence of Devon foliage, sea and sky has been distilled and given spiritual meaning here.

Dom Charles told my husband recently how modern stained-glass windows are made. Apart from some small pieces, the old method of enclosing the glass in lead has ceased to be used. Large church windows are now usually built in sections averaging six feet by three feet in aluminium frames. The glass is made elsewhere and comes in tablets twelve inches by eight inches by one inch thick which are then cut up in appropriate small cubes with a chisel hammer, the rough edges serving as increased reflexes of the light passing through like a prism. These fragments of many different shades of colour are laid out on a table, with a waxed underlayer within the aluminium frames according to Charles Norris's design, and then a plastic/asphalt melted compound is poured in between the glass pieces, which when cooled and set holds the whole creation in position.

Buckfastleigh Mills were important and working until fairly recent times and some of the mill buildings are still solidly impressive. Crafts are in evidence here as elsewhere, there is a display of fine work at the Dartmoor Craft Centre, and two potteries.

Also at Buckfastleigh is the John Loosemore Centre for Organ and Early Music; it combines an organ building workshop, teaching studio and recital hall in its premises, previously the Congregational Church in Chapel Street. It receives support from Dartington. A different kind of craft is pursued in the preservation and repair of old steam engines and rolling stock at the Dart Valley Railway Station, also at Buckfastleigh. It is a flourishing centre for railway enthusiasts and an excellent place to visit with your younger guests, to take the summer trip to Totnes and back by steam-train.

Dean Prior and South Brent

Not much more than a mile along the A38 west of Buckfastleigh is a group of houses and a church that form the hamlet of Dean Prior. Its claim to fame is that it was the despised home and cure of the poet Robert Herrick (1591–1674). He was a Londoner, not a Devonian, who in youth was an enthusiastic and witty member of the tribe of Ben Jonson. He took up the living of Dean Prior in 1629, "went into banishment into the loathed West", as he put it, was displaced by the Parliamentarians in 1647 but reinstated after the Restoration, and remained in Devon until his death; but his life as a country parson was certainly not unproductive, especially in the early period, as he admitted, despite the tedium he complained of:

> More discontents I never had
>   Since I was born, then here;
> Where I have been, and still am sad,
>   In this dull Devon-shire;

Yet justly too I must confesse;
 I ne'er invented such
Ennobled numbers for the Presse,
 Than where I loath'd so much.

Obviously it was personal circumstances that coloured Herrick's view, although one sympathizes with him having to endure the particularly soaking kind of rain we can get in Devonshire. But it's the rain that produces the wealth of wild flowers and rich harvests of the fertile soil, that Herrick describes so beautifully, and so succinctly; tedium never made him a long-winded bore. The wild daffodils still grow in the South Hams, you can see them from the Dart Vale trains, and Herrick wrote about them in this admirably terse lyric:

Divination by a Daffadill
When a Daffadill I see,
Hanging down his head t'wards me;
Guesse I may, what I must be:
First, I shall decline my head;
Secondly, I shall be dead:
Lastly, safely buryed.

But there is no sign in the church or graveyard of Herrick's grave, nor that of his faithful maid, Prudence Baldwin, for whom he wrote this epitaph, so different from all the witty verses to the Julias, Antheas and Lucias whom he had long before urged to gather their rosebuds:

Upon Prew his maid
In this little Urne is laid
Prewdence Baldwin (once my maid)
From whose happy spark here let
Spring the purple Violet.

Unlike Herrick, his contemporary, William Browne of Tavistock, in spite of absences from his native place, at Exeter College, in travels abroad, and residence elsewhere in England, retained a deep affection for Devon. It is expressed in many mentions in his poetry, particularly in *Britannia's Pastorals*, a long and fulsome work to read through but delightful if dipped into. Far from thinking of home as "loathed Devonshire", he writes:

> Haile, thou my native soil! thou blessed plot
> Whose equall all the world affordeth not!
> Shew me who can so many crystall Rils,
> Such sweet-cloath'd Vallies or aspiring Hils:
> Such Wood-ground, Pastures, Quarries, Welthy Mines:
> Such rocks in whom the Diamond fairely shines:
> And if the Earth can show the like agen,
> Yet will she fail in her Sea-ruling men.
>
> (*Britannia's Pastorals*, II.3.)

Other writers born in this area were John Ford, the Elizabethan dramatist (1586–1639?), at Ilsington, and Charles Kingsley (1819–1875), at Holne; but, of course, he wrote about North Devon in *Westward Ho!*.

A few miles more towards Plymouth brings us to South Brent, a village like the town of Ashburton, that's retained a strong sense of community and continuity. The church, beautifully sited among great trees well raised above the River Avon that runs beside it, is built over an ancient trackway and exhibits 700 years of architectural history, beginning with the remains of the Saxon tower. Among its interesting features are an eleventh-century red sandstone font, a specially good example of many in the area, and a sanctuary ring on the outside of the ancient main door. There are a number of these preserved in Devon churches. Once the ring was in his grasp a fugitive could claim sanctuary, until, perhaps, he was dragged away. One vicar of South Brent seems to have been unable to avail himself of the custom, for some unknown reason on the Feast of Corpus Christi in 1436 he was dragged out of another door and battered to death by a group of men.

The manor of Brent belonged to Buckfast Abbey from the eleventh century until it was acquired in 1546 after the Dissolution by Sir William Petre of Torbryan. Brent was an important centre for markets and fairs, serving its own extensive parish stretching far up into the moor as well as covering a big area of the South Hams. The annual Brent pony fair brought buyers from much further afield. The ponies of Dartmoor, used in the past for agriculture and mining, and more recently as excellent children's ponies, have for centuries been rounded up in a "drift" and selected stock sold. There is no longer a pony fair at Brent, although these still take place annually at Tavistock, Ashburton, Hatherleigh and Chagford.

Brent was declared a borough in 1556, and was later an important milltown; some of the mills are still working in fine solid buildings. The Old Toll House still stands with its board exhibiting the schedule of tolls levied on animals penned and stalls erected in the market-place, including bulls, caravans and donkey carts, dated 1889. As at Ashburton, there is much silvery slatehanging in the town. When Celia Fiennes, on her energetic tour of Britain at the end of the seventeenth century, saw slate-hung houses, she remarked: "The tiling is all flat, which with the lime it is cemented with makes it look like snow, and in the sun shining on the slate it glisters."

South Brent was the railway junction where passengers using the branch line from Kingsbridge changed to main line trains for Plymouth and Cornwall, or Exeter and upcountry. The Great Western Railway had reached Brent in 1848 but it was not until 1893, after decades of planning and delays, that the ten miles of "The Primrose Line", as the branch was called, were opened, with one thousand free tickets for local passengers for the first return excursion ride from Kingsbridge to Brent. Sixty years later there was a farewell turkey dinner on 10 September 1963 to commemorate the life of this branch line, surely one of the most idyllic railways in Britain. I can just remember travelling on it on one of our first visits to Salcombe. The train, drawn by a steam engine that puffed along at a leisurely twenty miles per hour, stopped at the several small halts. It was thrilling to go through the darkness of Sorley Tunnel, constructed with considerable difficulty because of springs under the hill above Kingsbridge. Now brush and undergrowth have grown over the rail-less track so that it is no longer even a pleasant walking path; and during the summer the roads are clogged with cars and coaches; although it must be admitted that the new express coach service from Plymouth to London is better than questionably efficient high speed trains. And the primroses are still there, earlier than anywhere else in England and blooming before Herrick's daffodils.

SALCOMBE SHIPYARDS A CENTURY BACK

Imagine doing it now! Fairly impossible
without juggernauts, tankers, aircraft, computers;
but they did. Brought the upcountry timbers by cart
from forests where man, horse, rope and labour

had felled and hauled enormous hearts of oak.
They needed them, struggling through red miry lanes
to the yards. From Kingsbridge and Dartmouth ropewalks
the coils, hemp sinews and muscles, came

down-estuary. In the sail-lofts, near
the Ferry Inn, great canvas triangles were sewn
by strong hands and needles. Imagine six yards
building three-masters here, a real-life scene

of real work. Ships grew so large
that one bowsprit stretched quite across
the street, in through a bedroom window, and
cold comfort for that sleeper caused!

Ships and families were born, grew, lived and died
together then, nourishing each other.
At night in the Union or Victoria Arms
talk was of cargo, voyages, drowning, disasters:

three hundred ships might shelter here from storm;
imagine them, and also the halcyon days,
the sun on sails homing to these safe shores
where aloes and myrtles grew and the air as now was warm.

Chapter Seven

THE SOUTH HAMS HEARTLAND

THIS ANCIENT REGION of the county forms a broad blunted peninsula bounded by the sea, the rivers Dart and Plym and roughly defined on the north by the A38 road. It is indented by the Salcombe–Kingsbridge ria and the Avon, Erme and Yealm rivers. The geological sandwich north to south of meadfoot beds, Dartmouth slates, meadfoot again and the coastal schists is a mostly low-lying area protected on the north by the rising steps to the moorland plateau and on the south by the slight upturn of the schist belt. This height increase that creates the towering seacliffs also enables their summit to be seen from a great distance inland, and the houses on the topmost road at Salcombe, and Malborough church spire, to be picked out long before the descent into Kingsbridge.

Guarded by bordering moors and seacliffs and watered by its rivers, streams and springs, the South Hams is an agricultural region of small farms, of on average a hundred acres, hamlets, some country houses and smaller estates, villages, towns, the ports of Dartmouth and Salcombe and the harbour of Newton Ferrers. Areas of managed woodland are small but significant, and include the Dartington woodlands, but everywhere there are woods and trees. Although the colours of nature may not be as startlingly vivid as they are in Cornwall, plant life is especially blessed in this area, and the normally mild climate allows sub-tropical species like palms and eucalyptus to grow happily. The grass really is greener and everything at least two weeks earlier than up-country in spring. Even in hard winters you can find pink campion in flower all the year round, and primroses and sweet violets out in January or February in sheltered places. In late October I have seen the last golden hazel leaves struggling to release themselves from branches where next spring's fat and fully-formed catkins are hanging.

The gentleness of the rounded whaleback hills sometimes ends abruptly in steep slopes that make tractor driving hazardous, and numerous small fields can be used only for rough pasture. Mixed farming used to be the norm, and dairying with the red South Devons and South Hammers, as big almost as buffalo, was traditional until the advent of more all-purpose cattle breeds like Hereford and Charolais spoilt the perfect colour scheme of green pasture, red or rich brown soil and chestnutty cattle. Now farmers tend to specialize either in dairying or corngrowing, and pigs are bred intensively. The land is rich and can support a lot of stock, so even small farms are profitable. In recent years some farmers have gone over to market gardening and self-pick crops of fruit and vegetables, especially in the rich-soiled districts of Charleton and Stokenham.

Will and Molly Moore farm thirty-six acres at Mill Farm, South Milton, near Thurlestone, in the district where Will's family have been farmers for many generations. Although the basic shape of the landscape is unaltered, they have seen enormous changes in almost half a century of farming. It is only four generations since South Devon oxen were used for all the work on the farm; when they were replaced by horses the blacksmiths' trade boomed. But the sizes of farms have altered as some farmers reduced their land by selling fields that had belonged to their holding since Saxon times, so that others increased their acreage. Big corngrowers have ripped up hedges and banks to make larger fields, although much less here than elsewhere, and now only where it is considered essential.

There are far fewer cattle markets, the largest one near the South Hams is now at Newton Abbot. Cows are sold privately rather than taken to market. The management of stock has changed as well. Will can remember the drift, when cattle were driven up to summer pasture on the moor, to save the farm grass for hay. "That was a good old chuer," he says, that took two days both ways. Now they are often kept under cover in winter in "mootels", as are sheep, with mass lambing in barns, which makes the shepherd's life a lot easier.

Life in and around the farmhouse has seen great changes too. In the past the farmer's wife had all the indoor work to do, with no hot water until she had boiled it over the fire she had kindled. She worked in the fields with the men, cooked for the labourers as well as her family, tended garden and poultry, made butter and cream to sell at the pannier market for her pin-money, and raised the calves. She may still do this. "A wife who is good with calves is the best assurance of profit," says Molly, remarking that it is perfectly easy to hand-feed twenty calves a day! But now wives are full partners with their husbands. Farm secretaries are no longer the rule and the farmer's wife does the accounts, often having had a secretarial or agricultural college training. Where in the past trade representatives would call at lunchtime to be sure of catching Mister, they now do business with his spouse. She drives the car-of-all-work, is again keeping a few hens and pigs and making cream, and her relaxation may be at WI meetings, the theatre, or nightclubs in Torquay. Now she and her husband often cultivate a popular summer cash crop: a field sown with caravans, and paying guests.

Many farmers' children want to farm (both Will and Molly's sons have followed their parents) but it is hard to get tenancies, most fortunate are those who inherit the family farm. There is a disturbing trend in this area for farms to be bought up by big estates and insurance companies and run from offices with a working manager.

Will and Molly are agreed that it is a good life, despite the tie and constant hard work and responsibility. Molly herself writes weekly farming articles on a huge variety of subjects for the local newspaper as well as working on a novel about historical farming life. "There are few people who would want to give up farming," she says. "You feel that the farm's your life and the life is the farm." Farming in Devon is as ideal a way of life as any, with its independence that offsets the unending demands of stock and land, and its peaceful setting. There may often be little time to observe natural beauties, but many are aware of them: the seasons' progress matching the work, not least illustrated in the hedgebanks of the lanes daily traversed by tractor and Land-Rover: the early spring feathering of cow's parsley, ferns and grasses, the primroses, tall shiny lime-green Alexanders, the spicy-smelling medieval pot-herb that grows three feet tall on its solid furrowed stems that taste like celery, topped with lemony-coloured flowers; it is replaced by drifts of stitchwort and small aromatic plants like pungent Herb Robert, salad burnet and the common catmint as well as the taller ranks of hogweed, hemp agrimony and meadowsweet, and the blues of scabious and harebell. The fragrance of the plants and the spicy air make drawing a breath in Devon a pleasure.

In winter the grey-green of old grasses and emerald of winter wheat stand out against the soft grey-brown of the woods, one of

England's loveliest muted shades. In them you see how their bones' green clothing is replaced by blue or grey as the sky's canopy replaces foliage.

All over the region the spokes of the lanes' web run from farms and from villages with their dreaming churches to converge on the towns, that although no longer markets in the old sense are still fuelling points and meeting places throughout the South Hams.

Dartmouth

Whether you arrive at the town from the west, where the road from adjoining Townstall dives straight for the waterfront, or the east via the equally steep but more curving road to Kingswear on the opposite side of the estuary, and then cross on one of the floating bridges, Dartmouth is captivating, with painted and stone houses climbing its hills by narrow lanes and alleys, and cuffed and fringed with woods along the river's cleave to the sea.

The arms of the harbour have enfolded grateful mariners from the beginnings of seafaring. Dartmouth was originally three separate settlements, the highest, Townstall, being the first one. It was rare for the early settlers to build right on the water, for fear of invaders. Clifton and Hardness lay to south and north of an inlet running in west of the main channel, for centuries called the Mill Pool. This was infilled during the seventeenth century. But the town, not merely the river mouth, had been known as Dartmouth since the thirteenth century. Much earlier than this, St Petrox, a Celtic saint, had a small chapel erected to him after his death in 594; a monastery was built on the site, within the castle precincts on the west bank at the entrance to the estuary, from the eleventh century onwards, and later a stone-built chapel, enlarged in the seventeenth century.

The first important event in the town's colourful history was the sailing of the second crusade from Dartmouth in 1147, then the third crusade in 1190. In the same century the harbour was busy with ships loading Totnes cloth for export and unloading wines from France and Spain, booms that lasted for a couple of centuries. The man who did most to consolidate Dartmouth's prosperity in this period was John Hawley; his ships combined with those of

Plymouth to form a royal squadron of privateers to control the
Channel and plunder French shipping. Later Hawley played an
important part in the building of the first Dartmouth Castle and
church and in organizing the customs, and was one of the two
borough MPs. The jingle attached to his name is still quoted:

> Blow the wind high, blow the wind low,
> It always blows fair to Hawley's Hoe.

Chaucer went to Dartmouth in 1373 on customs business and to try
to calm the enthusiasm of the Dartmouth mariners for taking
prizes, and it is thought that his portrait of the English seaman in
The Canterbury Tales was modelled on Hawley, whom he must
have met:

> A Schipman was ther dwellyng fer by weste:
> For ought I wot he was of Dert-e-mouthe.
> He rode upon a hackneye, as he coude,
> In goune woolen falling to the knee.
> A dagger hangyng on a lace had he
> Aboute his nekke under his arm adoun.
> The hot sumer had made his hew al broun;
> And certeinely he was a good felowe.

Hawley died in 1408; his effigy in brass is in St Saviour's Church,
whose building he largely financed. He stands athletically on a
hound, not in a woollen gown but in hose, helmet and armour,
sword at his side, between his two slim, graceful wives. His right
hand holds that of his second wife. It is a portrait of intense vitality
in a parish church containing idiosyncratic features. The south door
has extraordinary wrought iron decoration. The date 1631 is fixed
to the centre of the heavy oak door, and a bill of this date for smith's
expenses exists. But it may be that this was for repair or renewal of
existing work, for the design is strongly medieval. It depicts an
uprooted tree, the roots hanging down, with huge leaves. Over and
across this pace two strap hinges in the form of beasts: rather
lionesses than lions, for they have no manes, so possibly they are
leopards. I like it for the roughness of the execution as well as the
boldness of the design.

The church contains a sixteenth-century carved and painted rood screen and painted stone pulpit, a sixteenth-century communion table whose legs are figures of the four evangelists, and the arms of the mayors who owned the church and paid for its upkeep for 340 years, with those of recorders, medieval lords of the manor, and admirals of the fleets in which Dartmouth men and ships served.

The town was well defended on land as well as at sea in earlier times. There are castles on either side of the harbour mouth. On the Dartmouth side the strong square tower was finished in 1494. From the tower a permanent chain was stretched across the harbour mouth and fixed to a slit in the rock above water level near the ruined fortified house of Godmerock, that was superseded by the tower of Kingswear Castle in 1502. During World War Two a modern boom of steel cable, nets and timber blocked the entrance to the harbour, and similar defences were put across Salcombe and other harbour mouths.

The third castle is at Bayard's Cove, Bearscombe Castle, built in 1537 as a part of Henry VIII's coastal defences. Its site, which has a restricted field of fire, is not particularly suitable, and it was never used. But its masonry is so massive that it looks formidably permanent. Beside the Old Quay here was moored the *Mayflower*, which with the *Speedwell* had to put in first to Dartmouth and then to Plymouth after sailing from Southampton in 1620. Bayard's Cove's latest claim to fame is its use as a set for Liverpool Docks for *The Onedin Line* television serial, when the *Charlotte Rose* was one more famous ship to anchor in the harbour.

Until the beginning of the fifteenth century Dartmouth was the fourth richest town in Devon, after Exeter, Plymouth and Barnstaple, but after Hawley's death its fortunes declined for a couple of centuries. Then, after the great explorers Humphrey Gilbert and John Davis, whose homes were beside the Dart, had opened up the way to the Newfoundland fishing trade, another era of prosperity began, which lasted until towards the end of the seventeenth century. It was also enhanced by the renewed export of cloth from Ashburton carried down the Dart. Now came the second great period of building, of merchants' houses, a fair number of which survive.

Between 1634 and 1640 the Butterwalk was built, one of the finest examples of seventeenth-century Devonshire domestic architecture. The four adjoining houses were designed and built by

Mark Hawkings. The main living-rooms were at first-floor level, and the end house nearest the harbour has a fine view of the shipping. The upper floors were reached by the typical spiral staircases around wooden newel posts that may have been intended for ship's masts. They are still furnished with trip-steps, stairs of uneven height designed to trip up thieves and arouse guard-dogs.

The rooms are lighted by leaded windows, good panelling remains and, best of all, the marvellous plasterwork on ceilings and overmantels that reaches some of its finest flowering in the merchants' houses of Dartmouth. One overmantel depicts Pentecost, another the Judgement of Solomon. In the upper room of the house now a chemist's shop at No. 12 is an incredible plaster ceiling illustrating the Tree of Jesse, with almost fifty carvings of saints, prophets, flowers and budding leaves in circular tendril frames. Some of the figures appear to be sitting on swings amid their leafy surroundings, legs crossed, hands clasping vertical branches.

The house nearest the quay contains the Town Museum with an excellent collection of maritime models and pictures and objects from the town's history. The outsides of the Butterwalk houses, as also of several others in the town, are decorated with carved wooden creatures in fantastic shapes, cherubs, grotesques, lions, horses, human figures and foliage, secular not sacred subjects. As in other towns, Dartmouth architecture needs to be appreciated with a craned neck.

Despite plans to make Dartmouth a naval base in the seventeenth century and a shipping terminus in the nineteenth, it never regained its former maritime greatness. Today there are various small industries, including boatbuilding and fishing, but the greatest is the holiday trade. The busy harbour is a constant attraction. The Tall Ships race has started from here, yachts and pleasure boats arrive and leave and the Naval College craft add to the traffic, with the two ferries or floating bridges.

Situated on Mount Boone rising due north of the town centre is the somewhat bleak block of Britannia Royal Naval College for the education of naval officers. The college was established at Dartmouth in 1863, at first in old wooden ships moored in the harbour. Then in 1905 the cadets moved into the purpose-built college, where sixteen-year-old entrants have a university education as well as their preliminary naval training.

After Hawley, Gilbert and David, Dartmouth itself seems to have been its own leading personality. But one citizen became celebrated, the engineer Thomas Newcomen, 1663–1729, who took over the patent acquired by Thomas Savery of Modbury for a steam engine. An example of his engines is on display in a specially erected building next to the Royal Avenue Gardens.

Dartmouth has another museum, "Dartmouth's First Museum in the Ancient Workshop", which offers particular charm for two reasons: one, that it is a visual biography of an unusual and admirable man; the other that it has not been modernized but is as its creator worked on it and to a certain extent left it. Certainly it is crammed with objects, unlit and with numerous exhibits uncatalogued. But there is something in this that is more moving than a re-creation. So I find, who am constantly filled with gratitude to modern museum designers.

William Cumming Henley (1860–1919) spent most of his life in Dartmouth. Like Newcomen he served an apprenticeship to his father, in tinsmithing and ironmongery, and practised the trade in his home town, apart from the twelve years he spent in Torquay. Then he took over his father's shop. Henley had no schooling after the age of twelve, but he was a tireless autodidact, teaching himself languages, architecture, botany, natural science and the use of a microscope; he made a large collection of slides, was a proficient cabinet-maker and carpenter, and a gifted painter and etcher. After his death his sister arranged his collections in his workshop with its open upper loft approached by a wooden ladderway. I was greeted there by an old friend of the family, Mrs Uphill, the acting curator. She showed me the exhibits, books, tools, scientific instruments, models, above all pictures and photographs. It is a unique record of vanished Dartmouth, for Henley painted and drew scenes from the Dartmouth he lived in and also copied older pictures. He must have had phenomenal energy, and never shirked the long hours behind his counter; a poem he wrote gives a good-humoured impression of the frustrations he suffered; its first three verses run:

> Little drops of oil;
>   Little bits of wick;
> Pennyworth of nails;
>   Tin of scouring brick.

Ring of binding wire;
   Lamp burner gone queer;
I've called in to inquire
   Do you grind scissors here?

Box of black tinned tacks;
   Penn'orth of wire clout;
"Please to mend the kettle,
   Leaks around the spout."

There was clearly no end to it. His recreation was to walk the surrounding countryside and sketch, and then retreat to his studies.

The museums stay open in winter. A cold December day of bright sunshine allows you to look better at a town that in summer is packed with visitors from land and sea. In winter you can feel the continuity of Dartmouth's long life. People are painting the inside and outside of boats and houses, maintenance work of all kinds is going on. Lobster pots are piled on the quayside, boats lie up or snug at anchor. Residents stop to gossip in the quiet streets and have time to relax in their own pubs and restaurants.

Totnes

In summer on Tuesday market days the people of Totnes put on Elizabethan dress; their ruffles and laces, satins and velvets, breeches, full skirts and feathered hats blossom against the old houses, some with Tudor gables that are the final decorative layers covering medieval and later building stages. And they welcome you: never were there so many gurt big zmiles as among the Totnesians. Perhaps more than in any other town in the region Totnes offers a sense of history, and an organic unity that has grown naturally in the hillside space between the castle and the River Dart.

From the A38 Totnes is six miles from Buckfastleigh along the Dart. At first the road accompanies both river and railway: the Dart Vale Steam Railway that takes visitors for trips between Buckfast and Totnes, where in spring wild daffodils cover the riverside banks. Above the valley the hills swell steeply, with big grey farmhouses and their massive barns and outbuildings perched on green platforms up snaking lanes. From the hilltops the rolling course of the whalebacks south-east towards Torquay is evident, some green, some glossy crimson after autumn ploughing, or golden before harvest, and a few crowned with woods.

I like to approach Totnes from the Kingsbridge road to the south, to round the bend on the hill and have revealed in the foreground the upper town dominated by the crenellated castle keep, the church below it to the east and the rest of the little town lower still, with the newest development further away on the eastern hillside. A mile to the north Dartington Hall can be seen in its woodlands, and far against the sky the blue background of moor, in its centre the rough towers of Haytor. Whatever the weather this is a pleasurable view. There's a layby on the right where you can stop to see it at leisure, perhaps hear the church bells ringing over the Dart Valley, see a train far below going east towards Newton Abbot or west to Plymouth, and at night all the lights of the little town.

The centre of Totnes has retained the shape of a medieval walled town more distinctly than the port of Dartmouth, which has always been slightly larger and without walls. The first record of Totnes dates from the tenth century and the reign of King Edgar, when it was minting coins as a royal *burh*, having taken over this function from what is now the very small village of Halwell, to the south, earlier one of four Saxon boroughs of Devon set up by King Alfred chiefly for defence against the Danes. The other three were Lydford, Barnstaple and Exeter.

After the Conquest, William granted Totnes and over a hundred other manors in Devon to a Breton, Judhel, who became known as Judhel of Totnes. He probably built the first castle and founded a Benedictine priory as a cell of Angers Abbey about 1088.

What remains of Judhel's castle are his earthworks, the fine motte and bailey. From the mound there is a wide view over the town and the Dart, the route by which sea-raiders could advance. The shell keep, whose red sandstone walls stand so sturdily today, was probably built early in the fourteenth century, with its retaining walls and the town walls as well. The town map clearly shows the existing east and north gates and the position of the south and west gates, and the little rectangular medieval town with rounded corners. As the prosperity of Totnes increased – it was the busiest centre of the wool trade in the region – it overspilled its walls and grew down the western hillside towards the river. But Totnes, unlike Exeter and Ashburton, does not seem to have taken part in the development of the serge industry in the seventeenth and eighteenth centuries, and perhaps because of this it has always retained its air of a market town.

The Priory buildings near the church were demolished soon after the Dissolution. On the site was built the Guildhall, with the town prison in its cellars. It is a fine little building with some beautiful plaster work and is still used for mayoral functions; the old mayor-choosing ceremony was started up again in 1977.

The monks of the Priory, as well as running the parish church, their own chapel, a hospital, grammar school, lands, and in the fourteenth century keeping horses, dogs and hawks, administered the Lazar or Leper House of St Mary Magdalene, on the south side of the town. This was sited on the present Maudlin Road, and not far from the Leechwell, or healing well, along a lane with high stone walls. In the medieval period maudlin was the name for a leper hospital that also took in other outcasts such as prostitutes. Leprosy was widespread then throughout Europe, and the Totnes hospital was founded as early as the end of the twelfth century, soon after that of Exeter. Leland wrote: "Ther is an Hospitale by the Chirch Yarde; [and] ther is a Lazar House on the south part of the Toun . . ." It had a hall, chapel and accommodation for eight lepers, and functioned until about 1660. The Leechwell still flows from a deep underground cave source into three ancient stone troughs. Were the lepers, otherwise a segregated community, allowed to pass between those high walls to bathe in the healing waters of the spring? The ancient mysterious place holds its secret, I felt, when I walked round Totnes one cold February day.

The lanes here, that run parallel with the main street, cannot have been widened since their first making. This was the old road that climbed up the hillside on its way to villages like Ashprington or Cornworthy and on to Kingsbridge. At the bottom are the great old wharves and warehouses of St Peter's Quay (there was a chapel dedicated to him here). Once they were teeming with workers loading and unloading woollens, corn and other produce, and exchanging cider for wines and foreign goods. Some are crumbling now, awaiting restoration, but part of the quayside has modern warehouses where Reeves the timber-merchants keep their stores of sweet-smelling wood, some imported by sea from Scandinavia.

I walked along the riverside to the Plains, an open space taken up now with car- and coach-parking, past the memorial to John Wills (1843–1861), the Totnes man who with Burke was the first to make a crossing of the Australian continent, but died on the return journey. I crossed the bottom of Fore Street where it is traversed by the road to Dartington and the town bypass and where a right turn across the bridge leads to Torbay and Newton Abbot, and went into the Seven Stars Hotel through its handsome porch with the inn escutcheon incised in one of the stone flags, which are continued in the outsize hall, once the open courtyard of the inn. The building dates from 1660, and in its existing form was designed by the builder of the Seymour Hotel on the far side of the bridge. The sash windows are unusually large and elegant and these two white buildings graciously stand one on each side of the Dart. Defoe stayed at the Seven Stars and enjoyed a modestly priced dinner of salmon peal caught by the landlord from the river with the aid of a large net and a nippy dog that chased the fish into it.

I turned left up Fore Street, that rises more and more steeply up the hillside topped by the castle, looking up at the eaves, particularly those of the left-hand side of the street. Below them almost every house has a different moulding, giving additional variety to the shapes and colours of the houses. Most of them have seventeenth-, eighteenth- and nineteenth-century façades superimposed on the predominantly fifteenth- and sixteenth-century merchants' houses. I always enjoy walking this street, noticing something new every time, a cornice, an archway, a glimpse of plaster carving, a fresh angle or view.

One of the first houses on the west side is a late eighteenth-century "Gothic" house in Bank Lane, set back from the street; it is black and white and its narrow windows are angular; but the back is a surprise, hung with the indigenous silver-grey slates that clothe many houses here, sometimes in pleasant patterned arrangements.

A little further up and also eighteenth-century is a red-brick house that used to be the Grammar School.

The museum, at No. 70 Fore Street, is sixteenth-century and restored from near decrepitude, a gable-end house like those at Topsham, their burgage plots behind what was often a frontage of only one room's width and a narrow passage, and that was extended as need arose back into the garden space. In Totnes, the front room was the shop, living-room and kitchen behind. The rooms on the upper floor of the two- or three-storeyed house would often be connected by a gallery running across the courtyard that separated the blocks. The museum has a fine courtyard, where the deep angles of the tall building have to be viewed with a craned neck. At the back is a fragrant Elizabethan herb garden.

No. 16, handsome in black and white, was the home of Nicholas Ball, MP for Totnes in 1584. A plaque on the wall states that from this house his widow Ann married Thomas Bodley, the great book collector who gave his name, and his books, to the Bodleian Library, Oxford. The story goes that Bodley, then a man of substance and a diplomat, was engaged in a game of chess with a rival suitor in the wealthy widow Ball's house; while his patron cogitated Thomas took the opportunity to go into the garden and do some brisk courting that gained him the promise of the widow's hand, and then resumed his game. Checkmate, as it were.

Another High Street house has two painted masks of Tragedy and Comedy on its front. This was the site of a theatre in the nineteenth century, but only occasionally used by visiting companies.

The grey hung slates contrast well with the soft red sandstone of St Mary's Parish Church, a little recessed from the street to which it stands broadside. The Guildhall is behind the church, and the "Ramparts Walk" to it starts by the East Gate. In the fifteenth century Bishop Lacey was a benefactor to Totnes Church, his arms are in the porch, and a bearded mitred head adorns the pinnacled tower proclaiming: "I made thys tore." Of the same period is the stone rood screen running right across the church before the chancel.

The line of the houses on the south side is broken by alleyways with small houses along them, each one a personality. Their tiny gardens, tubs and hanging flower baskets make them bright shafts contrasting with the blue-grey, pink and dove tones of stone and slate.

At the top of the hill is the Butterwalk, the covered way formed by the first-floor houses supported on ancient granite pillars as at Dartmouth, Kingsbridge and Plympton St Maurice. In one house John Tuckey runs a fine antique shop and has done much loving restoration on the building. I climbed the newel stair to see the front room on the first floor with its plaster ceiling; the plaster has been brought almost to the level of the ceiling by centuries of assiduous whitewashing. I also saw the back room at Hodges men's shop, with oak-panelled walls, and typical rough, massive, granite fireplace. These are often attractively asymmetrical, since granite is a recalcitrant material to work. I recall them in various places: in Totnes, Plymouth, Dartmouth, and Hanger Farm, Cornwood; they were a standard fashion, but each one has had its blocks of granite painstakingly carted – even pack-horse carried? – down from Dartmoor, dressed to the extent necessary, and set up as a family hearth. In Elizabethan times John Tuckey's house, with its long burgage plot, had its own dairy, gardens, barns, stream, orchard, ciderpress and probably brewery. The merchant's home was a self-supporting community.

Soon after the turning on the right into Castle Street, High Street takes a sharp bend to the left, and after passing a little square runs into Cistern Street, that climbs steeply to join the Kingsbridge road. Water was led from the spring in the hill above to the conduit or cistern below. The lane leading up this hillside is steep and straight, utterly rural, the town left behind in a couple of yards. Tradition calls it Roman Road, but this seems unlikely. It is surely an ancient packhorse track, with great slate slabs laid, or naturally positioned, to make some sort of hardcore, although it is deeply eroded and the red banks on either side twenty feet high in places, covered with hazel and brambles bearing huge blackberries. From the fields at the top there is a completely different view down on Totnes, the slope so steep that it forms an overhang that hides some of the town while other parts not visible from the road below are revealed. It is not unlike an Italian hill town with its tumble of tiled roofs; and, as everywhere in hilly country, each new viewing point gives strangely marked alterations in perspective.

★ ★ ★

The medieval bridge over the Dart at Totnes was rebuilt in 1828 by Charles Fowler, a Devon-born architect. Beyond it lies Bridgetown, a borough set up by the Pomeroy family in the thirteenth century. A few hundred yards along the Torbay road a left turn leads to Berry Pomeroy. Totnes is surrounded by country houses and castles set in woods or combes, but whereas Follaton on the old Plymouth road, now the offices of the South Hams District Council, Dartington and Compton are preserved, Berry Pomeroy Castle is the most romantic ruin in Devonshire. Huge rhododendrons line the long, ghost-haunted drive down, a few wrens, tits and finches scold, there are strong odours of damp and fox. Turning a corner, you come upon the castle. You have been walking downhill, but you are not in a valley bottom. That is still further down, lying below the precipitous beech-covered limestone cliffside beyond the ruins. The medieval castle, built on the site of an earlier manor house in the early fourteenth century by the first member of the Norman de la Pomerai family to live here, was well defended on its rocky platform, and had the great gatehouse and curtain walls and towers that remain, to protect it on the side away from the cliff with the Gatcombe Brook below. The unusual thing about Berry Pomeroy is that inside the great courtyard, Edward Seymour, Duke of Somerset, who acquired it in 1548, built a mansion. It was an extremely ambitiously planned house with many large windows, some transomed. There is enough left of the roofless building for the whole to be visualized: the vast hall, huge fireplaces, many rooms, kitchens and staff quarters. But it was never completed. John Prince, Vicar of Berry Pomeroy church, wrote about it in his *Worthies of Devon*, published in 1701, that "the honourable family of Seymour . . . built a magnificent structure at the charges. . . upward of twenty thousand pounds, but never brought it to perfection". But he gives a fascinating description, from records he saw, of some of the decorations: "The Apartments within were very splendid; especially the Dining Room which was adorn'd, besides Paint, with Statues and Figures cut in Alabaster, with admirable Art and Labour. . . . Many other of the Rooms were well adorned with Moldings and Fretwork – some of whose Marble Clavils were so delicately fine, that they would reflect an Object true and lively from a great distance."

Prince says that it was a good day's work for a servant to open and shut all the casements. "Notwithstanding which 'tis now demolished, and all this Glory lieth in the Dust, buried in its own Ruines; there being nothing standing but a few broken Walls, which seem to mourn their own approaching Funerals."

About two miles north-east as the crow flies from Berry Pomeroy is Compton Castle, in the parish of Marldon. This is a splendid example of a fortified manor house that has survived all vicissitudes and is still lived in by descendants of the builder, who erected a large part of the house that stands today before the middle of the fourteenth century. He was Geoffrey Gilbert, who married the Compton heiress, and built the house with solar, cellar and great hall. A century later the house was greatly changed and enlarged, a century on again saw the addition of machiolated towers. The house was the home of Sir Humphrey Gilbert, brother of Adrian and John and half-brother of Sir Walter Raleigh, whose mother was Katherine Champernowne. Humphrey declared Newfoundland an English colony in 1583; he met his death by drowning when his ship, the little *Squirrel*, sank, while Humphrey sat on deck reading, saying to his crew: "Courage, my friends: we are as near to Heaven by sea as by land."

Compton remained the Gilbert home until 1800, when it was sold. But the family bought it back in 1930, half-ruined. A wonderful feat of restoration followed; the house is now the property of the National Trust, although still Mrs Gilbert's home. Its immensely high walls, repeated in those of the garden at the back, declare impregnability; but inside it is a gracious home, beautifully furnished and surprisingly light.

Another house with a darker fate is Oldstone, in the parish of Blackawton, some eight miles south of Totnes. It lies in a deep wooded combe that plunges southward, down a stugged track once an elegant drive, among straggling shrubberies and tall, decaying trees. An air of the tragic dissolution of former glory broods over the place more strongly than at Berry Pomeroy. Oldstone is a typical Saxon site, southward-facing, sheltered and well watered by streams. From here a ridgeway road with wonderful views runs a straight four miles to the coast at Strete.

The ruined mansion is near a medieval farmhouse, believed to have been the barton that also served as a courthouse for Torre Abbey, whose Premonstratensian monks were presented with

Oldstone manor in the mid-thirteenth century. The farmhouse walls are the only certainly medieval remains here, various other ancient looking structures are probably eighteenth- or even nineteenth-century additions of the folly genre, interesting as examples of architectural fashion. But a large Elizabethan mansion stood here to which was added an eighteenth-century block. The earlier house was three storeys high and had a great hall with an enormous Perpendicular three-light window. It looks ecclesiastical but there is no proof of this.

After the Dissolution Blackawton manor was granted to Lord John Russell, who acquired much Devonshire property. Soon after 1605 it came into the possession of Andrew Cholwich, one of the old family who had lived at Cholwich Farm on Dartmoor since medieval times. They owned Oldstone until 1837, and added the eighteenth-century block with a Georgian front and Tuscan doorway whose frame still stands elegantly offering entrance to a space furnished only with nettles and rubbish.

Then the Dimes family lived at Oldstone in prosperous Victorian comfort, building up the neglected estate and employing a large number of village people. However, in the 1880s and '90s a series of disasters, some say following a curse, put an end to this idyllic country life. One daughter was killed out hunting, and in 1884 Laura Dimes, the youngest daughter of the house, shortly after contracting a clandestine marriage, was found mysteriously drowned in one of the woodland ponds, standing upright in the water with only her hat just visible on the surface. Although her husband was tried for murder no charge was proved against him.

Finally the house caught fire and burned almost to the ground. The family moved away and Oldstone remained in its roofless ruined state. It is a melancholy sight. A silage clamp has been built to one side, and inside the perilously-leaning ivy-hung walls are heaps and mountains of sand and hardcore. The great walled stable yard is full of old machinery, the place exudes an atmosphere of darkness even in sunshine.

But in spring the snowdrops planted by Victorian Mrs Dimes have spread to form white carpets, and the grass and primroses are as green and gold here as everywhere in South Devon.

Oldstone has several curious features. At the edge of the woods, once furnished with carriage rides and linked ponds with waterfalls,

long overgrown, is the arched entrance to a small stone-built
structure. Its rough Gothic walls are crumbling, but set into one
side of the archway is an engraved plaque:

> Within a wood unknown to public view
> From youth to age a reverend hermit grew.
> The moss his bed, the cave his humble cell
> His food the fruits, his drink the crystal well
> Remote from man with God he passed his days
> Pray'r all his business, all his pleasure praise.

So run the first six lines of Thomas Parnell's long poem *The Hermit*.
Parnell was an Irishman who came to England to join the literary set
of Pope, Swift, Addison, Steele and Congreve. *The Hermit* was a
popular success, for this was the age of the Gothic revival, when
garden design changed from the formal Italian style to the
romantic, wild and fanciful. Side by side with Capability Brown's
beautiful parks and gardens with their lakes and wide views
developed a baroque, often grotesque fashion for follies and
grottoes, among which were hermits' cells. Pope went in for this at
Twickenham and countless country landowners followed suit.
There were some genuine hermits, but numbers were on the
hire-a-hermit basis, not always successful. I would guess that what
we see at Oldstone may be the work of the eighteenth-century
Cholwiches. According to Colin Gill, an expert student of local
architecture, the little arched structure was the hermit's larder, to
which food would be brought him from the house. It is near a
stream and damp and cool. A narrow hollow way was dug from the
larder into the wood so that the hermit could fetch his meals unseen
from the house in order not to disturb his statutory solitude. Deep
in the wood beside the remaining large pond is the hermitage, in the
form of a cross, also with an arched entrance. It has been used as a
boathouse and now as a cattle shelter; the solitude feels as absolute
as any desert anchorite's cell.

  On the north side of the mansion is the Shell House, a stone
building whose interior walls were covered with shells stuck into
the mortar. They were prised off for souvenirs by GIs in World War
Two. This may be of about the same date as the hermitage. Several
other walls, mounds and underground works witness to a vanished

age of elegance, touchingly incongruous in the prosaic agricultural surroundings and sad ruins of Oldstone today.

Dartington

The turning for Dartington Hall leads off the Buckfastleigh–
Totnes road by the 1880 replica of the old parish church that
originally stood close to the Hall, where only its tower, con-
taining some Champernowne memorials, still stands. The winding approach opens out after the estate grounds are reached, and
the Hall itself is approached across a tree-flanked forecourt. As
you enter the main north courtyard by a small door in the great
portals of the entrance block, the full beauty of the buildings
catches breath and gaze. Immediately to the right is a huge,
graceful swamp cypress tree, nurtured by a hidden wellspring
beneath its roots, an apt symbol for Dartington and its activities.
To east and west are continuous ranges of medieval buildings,
originally living accommodation for high-ranking staff members;
those on the west have arched, open entrance porches; at night
they are lit unobtrusively and are the most welcoming doorways
I know. Ahead is the glorious complex of medieval entrance
porch with its clock tower and silvery bells, on the west the
Great Hall with its line of long windows and beyond it the main
residential block, on the east the huge reconstructed medieval
kitchens, now the dining hall.

The combined genius of medieval and later builders, the
silver-grey limestone and the dedication of modern restorers
have here created a living space to protect, stimulate and nourish
the human spirit. The Great Hall is on the grand scale yet admirably simple so that its features can be easily assimilated: the light
provided by the seven tall windows, the magnificent hammer-
beam roof timbers and the long massive fireplace. It accommodates with equal benignity concerts, readings and plays where
once banquets were held. Whether in summer or winter or on
nights when the moon makes the shadows of the great cedars
and oaks black lakes on the lawns and Shakespeare's words
sound fresh as the spring from the garden stage, Dartington's
genius informs the faces of all who stay with especial awareness.

Dartington Hall, the Saxon "farm on the River Dart", is superbly situated on an undulating green rise above a boldly sweeping bend of the river. It is a lusher and larger lowland repeat of the Holne Chase Camp position ten miles upriver. The ninth-century register of Shafetesbury Abbey shows that the Lady Beorgwyn exchanged her lands in Dorset for the manor of Dartington. Ten centuries later another lady exchanged her lands across the Atlantic for the estate of Dartington, joined by her husband who descended from landowners in Yorkshire. Dartington's life through the intervening centuries is a videoscope of English history in the natural and architectural setting that presents a triumph of continuity today.

Before Domesday, Dartington belonged to a Saxon, Alwyn, from whom it was acquired by William of Falaise, a Norman who held many other manors in Devon. From the twelfth to the fourteenth century the Fitzmartin family were the owners; then came the great days of Dartington's medieval life, then Richard II made a gift of it to his half-brother and adviser John Holand, later Earl of Huntingdon and Duke of Exeter. Holand extended the sizeable Fitzmartin house into one of the most magnificent medieval mansions to be built in Britain, whose chief glory was the great hall with its towered entrance porch. On the centre ceiling boss inside the porch is carved the personal badge of Richard II, the white hart, surrounded by the wheat ears of John Holand. It is easy to imagine splendour-loving Richard, riding roan Barbary, visiting his brother in their palmy days, when the stones and furnishings of Dartington, the dress and accoutrements of the royal party and their retainers and soldiery were glittering in all the colours of an illuminated manuscript, until Richard's return from his ill-advised Irish expedition led to his downfall in the person of Henry Bolingbroke and later the loss of the Duke of Exeter's head as well, in that "all-hating world".

After further generations of Holands, the estate was bought by Sir Arthur Champernowne in 1559. He built a new residential wing on the west side of the Great Hall, still known as the Private House, now the Elmhirst Centre. The Champernownes ran the 2000 acre estate until 1921, making further alterations and enlargements before they began a long losing battle against the decline of their fortunes. Art treasures and land had to be sold, then in 1921 the estate itself was put up for sale, and the house remained empty for several years. The roof of the Great Hall was open to the sky, it had been stripped off decades before by Archdeacon Froude, Vicar of Dartington and father of J. A. Froude the historian, when, acting as trustee, he had considered it unsafe. The courtyard was fenced and trenched and the medieval splendour was falling fast.

But lines of fate were converging whose meeting would spark off an extraordinary rocket of revitalization at Dartington. Leonard Knight Elmhirst was born in 1893, one of nine children of an old Yorkshire family. After Repton and Cambridge he went to work for the YMCA in Mesopotamia and India during World War One, then took an agricultural degree at Cornell University where he met Rabindranath Tagore, who provided further inspiration for Leonard's developing interest in social conditions. Leonard went to Bengal with Tagore and set up an institute of rural reconstruction for him. Together they visited China, Japan, Italy and South America. Leonard travelled extensively throughout his life, even in the busiest Dartington years, for conferences and numerous functions concerned with agriculture, sociology and politics.

While at Cornell he had gone to visit one of the leading benefactresses of New York to ask her to support a university project. Dorothy Whitney Straight was then a young widow with three children, whose father had left her a great fortune that she was determined to put to the most idealistic and responsible use. Largely self-educated, she was passionately interested in the arts. She and Leonard were drawn to each other through mutual attraction and interests, and in April 1925 they married. They had evolved a future project that would allow them to develop their ideas, and which has been variously termed "an experiment in rural reconstruction", "the revitalization of rural life", "rural regeneration", and "renewing the vitality of the countryside". The blending of their ideals and mutual devotion became a power-source that fuelled innumerable activities.

The experiment was to be undertaken in England, and Leonard came back first to prospect for a suitable venue. At his first sight of Dartington, despite its then dilapidated state, he was instantly captured by "the beauty of it all, and every fresh vista only seemed the more to recommend the handiwork of nature joined with the reverent hand of generations of men", as he wrote to Dorothy. She was equally enthusiastic and the purchase went ahead. A massive restoration programme was begun on the buildings, the results of which we enjoy today. Timbers from the estate woodlands were used to rebuild the Great Hall roof and work was started on the gardens.

To start with the chief idea was to open a school in order to achieve Leonard' and Dorothy's ideas on education. Leonard believed that mankind can be liberated through an education that would teach self-reliance, appreciation and participation in the arts, the best aspects of town and country combined and "a pervasive concern for the individual human being and his right to self-determination". He also felt that the scientific spirit can be a continual spur to progress.

There were four main principles in the declaration of the aims of the school: (1) the curriculum should follow from the children's own interests; (2) learning should be by doing; (3) adults should be friends not authority figures, and (4) the school should be a self-governing commonwealth. As they jointly declared: "For us it is vital that education be conceived of as life, and not merely as a preparation for life."

The prospectus of Dartington School announces, as it has from the first edition: "This school is for adventure." The history of the school, one of the earliest and most liberal independent progressive co-educational establishments, is well-known and prone to exaggeration of its more colourful aspects. One of its first pupils is Michael Young, Lord Young of Dartington, author of *The Rise of the Meritocracy*, initiator of the National Extension College, the Consumer Council, the Institute of Community Studies and the Elmhirsts' biographer. His account of his schooldays emphasizes the time he spent reconstructing motorcycles and neglecting the breeding of poultry which was his chosen specialist subject! This kind of learning by doing obviously worked.

Dartington School provides independent secondary education for the age group thirteen to nineteen. The younger children are catered for at Aller Park, another purpose-built unit. In true Dartington tradition the children have written their own prospectus, *Especially For Children*, in which they list a vast range of subjects and topics for study and write graphically: "Aller Park Junior School . . . is part of a much larger school so we can do lots

of different things. Nobody hits you and teachers don't keep guard
over you." One evening at the end of the summer term I saw a
boisterous procession of variegatedly clothed children led by a pied
piper teacher playing a saxophone skipping around the grounds and
buildings. The children said that it was their end of term party,
during which at least one teacher was destined for ducking in the
swimming pool.

Dorothy Elmhirst's interest in the arts was responsible for the
coming to Dartington of numerous internationally famous figures
in painting, dance, music, arts and crafts, whose influence was to be
permanent. In 1955 the Arts Department became the Arts Centre;
out of this evolved the Dartington College of Arts in 1961. This
department regards itself as a specialist arts institution of national
standing studying international themes, whose particular concern
is to make the arts more accessible. And as well as an Adult
Education Centre at Shinner's Bridge, a quarter mile away in
Dartington Village, there is the Devon Centre for Further Education, opened in 1963, based in the courtyard range opposite the
Elmhirst Centre. It organizes short residential courses on many
different subjects, and is an inspiring place to stay.

Dartington's experimental philosophy can be seen in two of the
estate woodlands. North Wood, on the home estate, is an area
where selective silviculture is practised, with experiments in
mixing tree species, allowing natural growth, and managed
development, giving an effect of great beauty. King's Wood near
Buckfastleigh is used for kitchen-garden forestry. Mainly quick-
growing conifers are grown on its steep slopes, unsuitable for
arable farming, where carpets of tormentil shine beside groves of
rose bay willow herb in the valley bottoms.

Perhaps the most striking feature of a stay at the Devon Centre is
a direct legacy from the Elmhirsts: the atmosphere of welcome
that, combined with good food and comfortable accommodation,
stimulates students to lively and productive discussion. Like the
Devon Centre, the gardens offer a welcome at all times of the year.
Unlike formally enclosed gardens such as Hidcote in the Cots-
wolds, Dartington's are a modern version of Capability Brown's
ideas and a part of the landscape, wide-open and spacious or
shadowed with trees and shrubs, their colours varied yet unobtru-
sive. One evening I walked down to the Dart where the Himalayan

Balsam was growing along the banks as tall as I am. Coming back up the Valley Field towards the medieval Tiltyard with the twelve tall yew Apostles ahead, the Hall's velvety stone glowing behind the great oaks, the slant evening sunlight goldleafed the brightness of the grass and illuminated the moment in a flash of grace.

Dorothy Elmhirst maintained her interest in people, the arts, religion and philosophy until her death in 1968 at the age of eighty-one; Leonard died in 1974 at eighty. But their energetic spirits are as vital as ever today. From 1926 onwards a huge range of projects were conceived and born; they included poultry and cattle-breeding, cider orchards, woodlands, forestry and furniture, the Conference for Agricultural Economics, the Research Unit for Political and Economic Planning, soil surveying, textile mills, sawmills, horticulture, ornithology, artificial insemination, art, music, architecture, philosophy, literature and publishing, design, machinery, building, banking and finance, food and retail shops. Every year saw a new venture or branch of activity and this is a continuing process, although inevitably slower now. Naturally there were along the way some complications and disagreements, some failures and difficulties. But there was always boundless enthusiasm. One of the most successful ventures has been Darting-ton Glass, first made in 1967. The factory is at Torrington in North Devon. During the 1960s the Dartington Trustees decided to extend their work of social regeneration beyond the area of South Devon to help the depressed north region of the county, whose population was declining; the glass is marketed internationally.

The energizing influence of Dartington is exerted, not only in the surrounding area where numerous groups and individuals practise arts, social skills and therapies as well as commercial industries, but nationally and internationally. The Elmhirsts' transatlantic spiritual clout transmits its power to all who seek to share in it, whether permanent members of the community or those who come for a short stay at this ancient yet most modern of places in its paradise garden.

Modbury

The medieval market town of Modbury developed from a Saxon

settlement. Its plan is similar to Totnes and Salcombe, with its church on a height standing guard over the little town that descends the hillside below to a hollow meeting place of valleys between high ridgeways, whose streams run westward to the River Erme. At the bottom, a sharp left turn of the A379 Kingsbridge–Plymouth road leads into Broad Street that at a right turn into Brownston Street becomes Church Street. These are the principal streets, their houses with long narrow burgage plots forming a conservation area. On the west side of Church Street substantial houses with late eighteenth- and nineteenth-century façades and gracious porches, homes of prosperous merchants, step up the steep rise in a beautifully proportioned terrace, varied enough to engage the eye at each passing, and washed in mediterranean colours. Opposite, above a raised pavement, the façades are smaller, and older, many of them slate-hung. It is a pity that some of these naturally pleasing surfaces have been painted, as have others in hilly winding Back Street behind them. But the sixteenth-century timbered Exeter Inn is the pride of this side of Broad Street, striking in black and white.

At the top of Church Street, on the west side near the church entrance, the great family of Champernowne lived at the Court House from the fourteenth to the end of the seventeenth century. It was severely damaged during two civil war skirmishes and was later demolished and the stone dispersed and sold for building material elsewhere. Scant traces of Court House, and perhaps the medieval Priory too, remain in walls near Modbury Church, and pieces of old heavy granite moulded stones in the lower, western area of the town are incorporated into newer buildings. There is a fireplace lintel in the pavement outside the White Horse Inn. These scattered remains made me think of how John Donne in the seventeenth century was wondering about the difficulties of human bodies coming together with all their separated parts at the Resurrection, when

> . . . every tooth to a severall place is gone
> To vexe their soules at Resurrection. . . .

When houses are resurrected irretrievable losses are made up with new materials, and it takes an almost divine gift on the part of restorers to recreate the original persona of the house. Some of those in Devon succeed. But the original creators of the house do often live on in their name, that supreme human sign, even when the house decays. One such is Fowelscombe in Ugborough parish, the vast Tudor mansion of the once great Fowell family, now a romantic roofless shell gripped by giant biceps of ivy.

Brownston Street's houses demonstrate the success of Modbury's wool trade, begun in medieval times and at its height by the sixteenth century. These merchants' homes were created with an imaginative variety of frontage styles. The imposing Old Traine House, an Elizabethan mansion, was replaced by New Traine House, which has an impressive nineteenth-century pillared façade. Chain House once had chains in front of it, and is a handsome three-storeyed town house with a portico and four dormer windows in the roof. Tall three-storeyed Brick House was a hat factory in the nineteenth century. What used to be the Modbury Literary and Scientific Institute founded in 1840 by Richard King, who made a fortune in New York, looks out of place, like someone in a pristine suit among easy but stylish country casuals, with its white façade, Tuscan porch and attached Ionic columns above.

The two Civil War battles of Modbury seem not to have been very serious affairs and the records are conflicting. There appears to have been a group of locals who took a mercenary view of the situation and would fight on either side, although tending to favour the Royalists, provided they were paid!

Some of the Parliamentary troops were billeted in the church, where they vented their savagery on the effigies, particularly those of the Prideaux family. One effigy is a mere torso, the other has had both feet hacked off. This had been a contentious place before Cromwell's time. The church on its hilltop has a fourteenth-century broach spire similar to that of Malborough. It incorporated the priory chapel of St George given by the Valletort family in 1140. It was a cell of a Benedictine Abbey in Normandy, from where the Valletorts originated. The church was shared between the Prior who was responsible for the chancel and the vicar and parishioners who had the care of the nave. The Prior could claim a larger share of tithes and there was bad feeling between the two parties: the vicar took to burying parishioners under the Prior's windows in the shallowest of graves. . . .

By the mid-fifteenth century the church had fallen into disrepair.

Then began the second great period of church building in England undertaken partly in gratitude for the cessation of the plague, partly because of civic pride and prosperity. The age of the Perpendicular style had come. Eton College became the benefactor of Modbury Church and is thought to have been responsible for extending the aisles and building the chancel. A fine peal of bells was collected, in which Modbury has always taken pride:

> Hark to Modbury bells
> How they do quiver
> Better than Ermington
> down by the river.

But during the first half of the fifteenth century interest in church building had begun to wane in favour of domestic architecture, and many large houses were built in England. Before this even the gentry were probably living in cob houses; now the masons were set to employ their skills on vernacular architecture and country houses. The Champernownes prospered and during the fifteenth century Katherine Champernowne married first Otho Gilbert and had her three famous sons, John, Humphrey and Adrian; then married again, Walter Raleigh, and became the mother of an even more renowned Devonshire celebrity, Sir Walter Raleigh.

The early importance of Modbury as a marketing centre is evidenced by the granting of its market in 1155. Bill Hingston the folk singer, born here, quotes: "When Plymouth was a furzy down Modbury was a busy town." Permission to hold a fair was granted in 1429. As at Kingsbridge and other towns, the opening of the fair was announced with the ceremonial hoisting of the white glove garlanded with flowers to symbolize free trading and leniency by the law while alcohol was on sale from street traders and private householders. The glove-raising is an ancient symbol still shown at the opening of the rather differently styled present-day fairs. It is said to commemorate a glove given by King John during his visit as a token of the charter he granted for the holding of the fair.

Another custom was the hanging of a holly bush outside the private houses that in fact served as "public houses", perhaps a reminiscence of the shrub's use in Saturnalian revels. People in the region used to have holly bushes instead of spruce for Christmas trees as well as singing the old carol about the holly and the ivy. Older beliefs linger on in the memory's subconscious; how many tourists realize that when they go to a ram roast they are participating in an ancient fertility rite?

At the market, the cattle and other stock were sold in Broad Street, the only level space in the town, until 1940; the final cattle market was held in 1944; but some of the old customs, including the Mile Race, were revived for the one-day annual fair now held in spring, when the Town Crier hoists the glove and flowers beside the old market bell that hangs on the wall of an antique shop, once the Bell Inn and earlier still Church House.

Bill Hingston was born in Modbury, although his home has been at Dittisham ("Ditsam" in the vernacular) for years now. As a young boy about ten years old he was set to driving the sheep. His father was a carrier, and Bill believes that many of the songs that were sung in his youth were picked up by the drovers and carriers as they went about the countryside, along the roads to the fairs. He sings his father's song that begins:

> For I'm a country carrier
>   And a jovial chap am I,
> I whistle and sing from morning to night
>   And all troubles I defy.

It was a hard life, but Bill remembers it as a good one too, and in some ways more full of plenty than today. There was never any shortage of firewood, for instance, and Bill's grandfather said that it didn't matter if they burned half a coppice a night; there was always plenty of good cider, and breakfast consisted of a thick round of bread, a generous dollop of clotted cream and treacle on top.

One of the great events of the year was the trip to another fair, the famous Tavistock Goosey Fair. Bob has his own version of the old song:

> Away we'll ride come Friday next
>   Bill Champernowne and me
> Off us goes in our zindy clothes
>   The goosey fair fur to zee.

Us washed and shaved a bit
   Us greased 'n combed our hair
And off us goes cross Dartymoor
   Behind the ole gray mare.

Fur 'tis all "'N where be gwuin
   What be doin all there?
Lay down yer prongs
   'N strap it along
Ter Tavistock Goosey Fair."

Us zmelt the sage 'n onions
   All the way ter Wychers Down
And didn' us have a blowout
   When we got in thiccy town.

There us met Ned Hannaford
   Jan Stewer and Nicky Square
It seemed ter me all Devon must be
   Ter Tavistock Goosey Fair.

Fur 'tis all . . .

Us went 'n zeed the horses
   The heifers and the 'oes
We went upon the roundabouts
   Into all the shows

And then it started rainin
   And the volks came droppin in
So us walked into the Bedford
   And 'ad a drop o' gin.

Fur 'tis all . . .

'Twas rainin 'ard and dark's a beg
   When us went 'ome that night,
And when us got round Merivale Bridge
   Th' ole mare 'er tuk a fright.

I zed ter Bill be cearful
  Or yer'll 'ave us in the drain
Bill zed ter me "Cor beggar", zed ee,
  Haven't *you* got the reins?

Fur 'tis all . . .

Jest then th' ole mare er caught 'er voot
  In some whackin girt big stones
'Er kicked th' ole trap ter flippets
  'N trotted off alone.

When us come till our recknin
  'Twas no use sittin there
'Cus us had thirteen mile ter walk
  Frum Tavistock Goosey Fair.

Fur 'tis all: "'N where be gwuin
  What be doin all there?
Lay down yer prongs
  And stap it along
Ter Tavistock Goosey Fair."

Folksong evenings when Bill and his friends are singing and step-dancing is in direct continuity with the spirit of the old fair. A pub is the normal venue and beer the usual drink now rather than cider; and after all, beer was the old drink in these districts, in the South Hams a fierce brew called White Ale. Risdon wrote of Modbury: "The town is noted for nappy ale, of which liquor, Henry of Auranches, an arch-poet in King Henry the Third's time, wrote thus:

Of this strong drink, much like to Stygian lake,
Most term it ale, I know not what to make;
Folk drink it thick, and piss it out full thin;
Much dregs therefore must needs remain within."

The songs, which are being recorded by Sam Richards and Tish Stubbs of Totnes, are variously historical, sad, bawdy and romantic, and the evening passes in a flash, until the landlord starts to look patient and someone at length says, "Ah well, time to bugger off," and we go out into the dark, fresh and fragrant lanes.

Modbury's history after the Civil War is a peaceful one, the only reminiscence of war still evident being the solid four-square stone enclosure at the north-east end of the town surrounding a space of four acres constructed as a barracks for troops mobilized for the Napoleonic wars, where they were billeted under canvas.

When you round the corner at the top of the hill past the wall of the barracks and the end of the town you see a ridge to the north with a spaced-out row of Scotch pines marking it like a stalwart line of defending giants, and probably planted by a nineteenth-century landowner to denote his boundary. There are three ridges running east to west, each bearing a prehistoric ridgeway leading to the lower reaches of the Erme. Bronze Age Beaker People probably landed there after crossing from the Continent and made their difficult way up to the less densely vegetated hills of Dartmoor to found their settlements, taking with them the few cattle they may have brought with them, or domesticating the indigenous wild ones. For many centuries after them South Hams farmers drove their cattle along the ridgeways up to the commons on the moor for summer pasturing, to save the rich grass of their fields for hay, and they renamed some of the ancient ways driftways. If you stop on a ridgeway, and they are quite numerous in the South Hams with its many hills, some of them still with widely-spaced hedges and verges, the sense of the past is strong.

The primitive cattle were bred over the centuries to become the beautiful South Hammers, the South Devons whose glossy coats match the red soil and whose slow generous shape suits the contours of the landscape so well. Until a few years ago a herd of them could be seen making their leisurely way twice a day along Brownston Street in Modbury to a farmyard behind one of the houses, whose barns and sheds still stand, used now as stores and garages. The farmer was forced to give up keeping his milking herd there when the lorries grew too big to get up the narrow alley entrance to collect the milk. But until then the cows in the street, taking precedence over motor traffic, emphasized Modbury's long history as a centre of farming.

A number of farms recorded in Domesday lie close to Modbury, with at least six names of mills near them. Great Orcheton belonged

to the Prideaux family, and there are Little Modbury, Spriddles-
combe, Yarnicombe, Stokenbridge, each beautiful and interesting. Oldaport is a fine example of a Devonshire cross passage
house, where the passage divided the shippon, or cattle shed, from
the living quarters. Today it is well cared for and the ancient
white-painted walls hung with modern paintings that suit the old
house well, just as medieval and modern music often go well
together. On a ridge beside the garden are the remains of some very
old walls with traces of the foundations of two towers. Traditional
reports that this was a Romano-British fort or settlement have not
yet been confirmed by excavation. "Port" could mean a market or
walled town, although this one is near the Erme estuary, which was
used for unloading lime and coal, and loading cargoes of tin and
wool, up to the end of the nineteenth century.

Kingsbridge

The best distant view of Kingsbridge is from a boat on the estuary;
from the top of Bolt Head it is hidden behind the rounded hills. But
ten minutes by fast motorboat, half an hour by a favourable breeze,
will take you from Salcombe to Kingsbridge up the ria on a rising
tide. The digitate creeks branch out to west and east: first, on the
west side, is Batson behind Salcombe harbour; then opposite on the
east is the beautiful stretch of South Pool creek, with its own small
inlets of Goodshelter and Waterhead forming small, snug anchorages. The narrow deep main channel north of these two is called
The Bag, where quite large yachts can safely moor. Here is the
mother ship and residential quarters for cadets, visitors and staff of
the Island Cruising Club, watching over flocks of novice smallboat
sailors.

Next, Frogmore Creek opens out to the east round the thickly
wooded corner of Halwell with its ancient heronry. From their
high roosts the pompous fisherbirds flap creakily round and down
to stand on the slate and mud shores to fish. On Ham Point halfway
up Frogmore Creek were some of the once-busy Charleton slate
quarries that supplied fine silvery-grey and pink material for
buildings as far away as Dartmouth. A score of ruined lime kilns at
various points on the ria shores witness to the time when ships

brought limestone from Plymouth or Berry Head to be burned into lime for the fields and for mortar.

The central channel now opens out into a broad area, Widegates, ideal for sailing. There is a raised bank near the east shore called Saltstone Rock that appears at low tide. During the persecution of the Nonconformists in the seventeenth century, ministers John Hicks and John Flavel brought their congregations here outside parish boundaries for services. Now the congregations are of gulls, oyster-catchers and curlews that forage on the rock and the neighbouring mudflats at low tide. From here Kingsbridge can be seen nestling on its ridge between two higher valley-sides, the spire of St Edmunds centrally placed with the lower part of the town dropping down to the ria end, a perfectly sited small city.

At the end of Widegates the deep channel snakes vigorously to its end a mile further, followed by means of marked posts. It is tiresome, not to say humiliating, to get stuck on the mud for the space of six hours waiting for the incoming tide to lift the boat again. We moor up on the east side of the channel past the remains of the old Date shipyards where schooners were built; and this is where the paddle-steamers that plied several times weekly between Kingsbridge and Salcombe, and the Plymouth packet boat, moored until the 1920s. Until the coming of modern roads, the sea was the better route. Now the moorings at the ria end are taken up by the Norwegian design with boats made by Wills Brothers, the present-day boatbuilders, but an old Devonshire family.

The latest Kingsbridge housing development on the hill above Dodbrooke to the east has not greatly encroached on the old Saxon layout. Salcombe historian James Fairweather called Kingsbridge "the metropolis of the South Hams"! There is no doubt about its continued urbanity and activity, proclaimed by the Town Crier with bell and three-cornered hat up and down Fore Street, winter and summer. For many centuries it has been the centre on which people from Salcombe and all the smaller surrounding villages converged to shop for household goods or attend fair and market.

Kingsbridge may have received its name on account of the royal estates adjoining the ancient town. There is no record of a single bridge, in Justice Hawkins's early nineteenth century there were six bridges over the small streams, now covered watercourses, which still flood the lower part of the town, especially Mill Street, after heavy rainfall or snow, almost every winter.

The early abbots of Buckfast recognized the advantages of this snug site at the head of the navigable estuary, and kept houses here for centuries; a granite archway is traditionally held to be part of the abbot's banqueting hall. Permission was granted for a market to be held here in 1219, and it has continued ever since. The town became a borough in 1238. The abbot's corn mill was in Mill Street where the last town mill still stands, empty and deserted but a striking building with its great swinging chimney cowl. The mill wheel was driven by water from leats, shallow trenches diverting the streams, that ran in curves around the east and west sides of the town. The one to the west still does, a sizeable, clean, busily-moving little waterway. Beside it is Western Backway, originally "backlet", a path between high walls, some of which were built by Napoleonic prisoners of war. There is an eastern backlet too; these and other narrow paths and alleys are pleasant to walk through. The original burgage plots end at right angles to the leat, some with gates opening on to it, bridged with great slabs of blue slate.

St Edmund's Church is originally thirteenth- and fifteenth-century, savagely restored, but it contains a fine Flaxman monument, and, on a slab outside, the epitaph of Robert Phillips:

> Here lie I at the chancel door,
> Here lie I because I'm poor,
> The further in the more you pay,
> Here lie I as warm as they.

Robert died in 1798, a quirky character, cooper by trade, who collected simples for medicines, and was the local whipping boy, accepting punishment as a scapegoat at a penny a time.

Before St Edmund's was built the Kingsbridge people had had an arduous task to bury their dead. As their petition for a church of their own, written in the thirteenth century, stated, they had to toil "up a high mountain" to Churchstow, the mother church to the north two miles away.

Between the encircling embrace of the backlet walls the town centre is bisected by steep Fore Street. The fronts of the houses are now mainly nineteenth- and twentieth-century, a few eighteenth, but behind some façades are sixteenth-century gables, and a fifteenth-century cruck roof has been recently discovered. In the alley between Nos 49 and 51, beside Donovan's furnishing shop, is an old granite archway that in the nineteenth century and probably earlier was the entrance to the Revd John Morris's Classical Mathematical and Commercial School where some notable Kingsbridge burgers were educated.

In 1586 a drawing on parchment was made of Kingsbridge. It was inscribed: "The trewe Platt of the newe byldyng, upon five pyllers of stone, betwixt the Church styles of Kingsbridge. 1586." It shows Fore Street, St Edmund's and "the Church yeard of Kingesbridge" and in the centre of the street facing it "The Cheape house of Kingesbridge". The drawing's slightly off-beat perspective shows modern-looking houses each side of Fore Street with their long, narrow gardens.

In 1796 when wheeled traffic was increasing and impeded by the old wooden market building in the middle of Fore Street it was demolished and the Shambles built for the butchers on the site of an older cornmarket. The granite pillars from the Cheape House were used for the Shambles and stand in the colonnade here today. There is still a butcher's shop here, although it is anything but a shambles!

To the south of the church is the town hall. It was built about 1850 in solid pleasing style, and intended for a wide variety of uses: a butter and poultry market, a drill room in winter for the 26th Devon Volunteer Rifle Corps, lock-ups and police offices, clubrooms, court-room, lectures, concerts, bazaars and even Sunday services held by some of the sects without buildings of their own. There was also a "commodious withdrawing-room", a reading room and a museum of stuffed birds. It houses various functions now, an excellent theatre, and markets run by different groups.

The town hall is surmounted by a particularly beautiful, compact clock-tower. The square, decoratively slate-hung base narrows in the beginnings of a spire for about a yard, above which the four round faces are fixed; above them is a small ball and a pawn-shaped top. A strange feature is the lack of a clock dial on the fourth side looking west. Of course it cannot be seen from the street, but it was in view from the workhouse on the ridge across the intervening valley. Was time considered irrelevant for those unfortunates? Or was this merely a matter of economy?

The shapes and materials of the town hall building, the church and the Shambles are an architectural unit that is most satisfying to view, in combination with the prospect looking south from this hilltop point, down the sweep of Widegates, glittering in the sun at high tide or surmounted by billowing cumulus repeating the forms of the rounded many-shaded hills, never unwelcoming even in rain and storm.

Dodbrooke, now part of Kingsbridge, was originally a separate town and was granted a market and fair at an even earlier date. The fifteenth-century church that replaced a chapel stands high on a spur. Although it did not grow quickly like Kingsbridge, in the nineteenth century the shipyard and quays were in its parish, an important edge-tool foundry and a large cattle market on the space near the old cinema, marked by an incised stone in the wall.

Towards the end of the eighteenth and throughout the nineteenth century schools proliferated in Kingsbridge and Dodbrooke, as elsewhere. There was nothing to prevent anyone, master or dame, setting up as teacher. The two leading ones were the Grammar School at 108 Fore Street, now the Cookworthy Museum, and John Morris's School. The Grammar School was founded in 1670 by the good Quaker, Thomas Crispin, a fuller and cloth merchant. He was born in Kingsbridge in 1608, moved to Exeter in 1630, became a prominent member of his trade, and was twice Master of the Weavers Fullers and Shearers Company. A life-size full-length portrait of him hangs in the museum, dressed in black kneebreeches and cloak, white stock and wide-brimmed black hat: a striking figure.

John Morris was a Quaker, and clerk to the Kingsbridge meeting for forty years. Among his pupils was the literary celebrity of Kingsbridge, John Wolcot, better known as Peter Pindar, satirist and author of copious works. His house on the quay, Pindar Lodge, still stands, but his beloved barn, to which he wrote an Ode and an Elegy, no longer exists. One of his schoolfriends was the first local historian, scholarly idiosyncratic Abraham Hawkins, JP, FRS. Good John Morris encouraged his pupils to write poetry as well as learn grammar and mathematics, and he was commemorated by

Abraham Hawkins in an elegy after Morris's death in 1788 at the age of seventy-one. Hawkins describes him as:

> Of morals pure and manners mild,
> Preceptor lov'd by every child:
> With mind possessed of classic store,
> The mien of meekness Morris wore

and says that:

> From his instruction Wolcot caught
> The spark that kindled radiant thought,
> Illumined paths that lead to fame
> And with the Nine enrolled his name.

Peter Pindar kept in touch with Hawkins after he left Devon, and in the *Elegy to my Barn* wrote:

> While Hawkins yields a plaudit to my song
> The Snakes of Envy hiss in vain at Peter.

Abraham Hawkins stayed in his native Devon, first as an officer in the North Devon Militia. Then he resigned, married and took up his inherited property at Alston, Malborough. He loved the house, describing it as "half unbosomed seemingly in a wood, over-looking ever-verdant meadows that reach the limit of the waves . . ." – the grounds slope down to Widegates.

Hawkins led a quiet but busy life as a country justice, riding to the Magistrates' Court at Kingsbridge and attending Quarter Sessions, and corresponding with Sir Thomas Acland the Member of Parliament on various points of legal and political interest. One of his letters from November 1813 expresses the frustration he suffered from his fellow magistrates:

> Were I to tell you half the dirty conduct . . . which I have witnessed in *city* and *borough* justices in the twenty-four years when I have acted as a magistrate for Devon, you would set me down as a Monkhauser!!! I may venture to observe, to you in a *private* letter, that these magistrates and counsels are mere tools in

the hands of *pettifogging* town clerks; and the *half*-education in law which the latter receive instructs them only to do dirty acts to save their own pockets or put money therein. . . .

Hawkins entertained Sir Thomas at Alston: "My house is ever at your service, *when* it falls in with your convenience of proceeding," he wrote. Alston is an unusual house, made up of three adjoined blocks from different periods, none later than the eighteenth century and mostly Georgian in appearance, but at the back there is a ruined block, originally three-storeyed and the oldest part. The present owners refer to it as "the Chapel" because of the frieze in relief that was carved on the wall above the fireplace. This has completely disintegrated, but the figures are known to have represented the sacrifice of Isaac, with scrolls above them proclaiming: "Hold, Abraham, hold thy hand; it doth suffice. Obedienc [*sic*] is more than sacrifice." Hawkins mentioned his "Justice Room" in letters, and is still remembered locally as having been a severe man, sometimes even referred to as Judge rather than Justice Hawkins. Probably this room is where he executed summary jurisdiction.

Today Abraham Hawkins would sigh "Sic transit. . ." if he saw his once elegant home, now the office of a large caravan site with a caravan squatting on his front lawn. The only unchanged element is the incomparable view over the estuary. Hawkins's lasting monument is his delightful history of Kingsbridge and Salcombe, published as a modest octavo volume in 1819 and dedicated to "John Wolcot MD long accredited at the court of Apollo as Peter Pindar Esq". Much valuable information is contained beneath the ornate curlicues of his baroque prose style.

Part of Abraham Hawkins's work as a magistrate was dealing with the plight of vagrants and paupers who roamed the roads and lived in appalling conditions. Various reports from the local newspaper tell the story of the second-class citizens of that time. Before the setting up of Unions of workhouses in the 1830s, each village had its own poorhouse, where the only poor relief, apart from that donated by wealthy ladies of the villages, was obtainable, and dreaded.

The Kingsbridge Union included twenty-six parishes of the South Hams, covering the area bounded by Thurlestone to the west, Modbury to the north and Stoke Fleming to the east. A new workhouse was built in Union Road in 1837 at a cost of £6,000. It was constructed in three storeys of brick and stone to hold 350 inmates; the average number was in fact eighty-three, so there was at least no overcrowding. The solid building still stands, grimly glowering on its rise.

Little is known of the first fifty years of the workhouse's existence, but in 1887 applications were sought for a Master and Matron who were to receive a salary of £40 and £20 respectively. Rations – an ominous term – and furnished accommodation were provided. One married couple held the posts for twenty-three years.

In certain respects the inmates received quite generous treatment, particularly in the matter of the clothes supplied to them. Men were given coats, waistcoats, trousers, shirts, shoes, stockings, hats and handkerchiefs; women had gowns, under-petticoats, upper petticoats, shirts, aprons, handkerchiefs, shoes, stockings, caps and bonnets. There was also an allotment of tobacco, and straw for bedding.

The diet sounds solid and adequate, if starchy, and vegetables were grown in the workhouse garden. For Christmas there was an allocation of oranges and a magic lantern show, and once in 1871 the workhouse was given a treat of fifty rabbits, perhaps some poacher's confiscated haul.

To celebrate Queen Victoria's Diamond Jubilee in 1897 the inmates were given hot roast beef and jam puddings for dinner, two ounces of extra tobacco, half a pound of tea, and sweets. On the other hand, in 1871 there had been a complaint about Australian imported meat that was discovered to be jackass and kangaroo. A discovery still being made in the 1980s!

There was a supply of cider, perhaps even white ale on special occasions; and a weekly ration of a pint of gin. In October 1869 two old women paupers were punished for disorderly conduct by having their gin ration stopped and their diet reduced to bread and water. The next report stated that their conduct had improved.

But despite these apparent comforts, it was a workhouse, after all, and the inmates followed the traditional occupation of picking oakum here as elsewhere. Probably the worst misery was the winter cold. In 1863 an inquest was held on a pauper child at the workhouse who had crept inside the fireguard to get nearer the meagre fire and whose dress had ignited so that she burned to death. In 1900 more coal was allotted for use in the room where aged people waited to receive weekly relief, as there had been complaints about the cold.

And not all the building was solid. In 1871 it was found that the vagrants' room was "unsuitable" because the roof was falling in. Vagrant boys were "trained" until they were thought fit to serve on farms, at sea, or put into general service at the workhouse. In the same year, 1871, there were no jobs available, so the clerk of guardians was directed to apply to the Admiralty to seek places for the boys in the Navy. Terrified, and no doubt recalling tales they had heard of conditions in the senior service, some of the boys ran away. But they were caught, brought back to Kingsbridge and put on bread and water for absconding.

The workhouse board of guardians' reports give accounts of the state of health of the inmates and of problems with disease and sanitation in the villages. The medical officer at the workhouse sometimes had to be taken to task for neglect. In 1866 the report notes that there had been "itch" in the workhouse, and a recommendation for more food, milk and stewed apples is made.

During the 1860s and '70s drainage and sewage works were being built in the villages, but conditions were still extremely unhealthy and hygiene unknown by the average village-dweller. There were outbreaks of cholera at North Pool, where the water supply came under suspicion, and smallpox at Salcombe, among other ills. The Salcombe people were reprimanded for their habit of throwing slops over the quay into the harbour – where the mud is not exactly sweet-smelling today at low tide. In 1867 the report stated that ninety houses at Salcombe were without "necessary accommodation" – the board's coy term for lavatories; the offending house-owners were ordered to erect "necessaries". However, at South Huish it was said that people had been throwing their slops out in front of their houses for the past 150 years, and the inhabitants were noted for their longevity; one man of eighty was still at work.

The depressing reports continue: there was typhoid in Kingsbridge where there had been complaints about failing to remove dung. The nurse at the workhouse had had to be sacked for drunkenness and the new one was insolent. In the Union hospital patients were sleeping on straw until flock or coconut fibre mattresses were ordered; and a woman was reprimanded for the "culpable folly" of going to Plymouth with two of her daughters to visit a third daughter dying there of smallpox. Vaccination was practised but not compulsory.

A last glimpse of workhouse life is an order given in 1877 to house an ailing man. He broke down on the long walk up Union Road and was assisted to the house in a wheelbarrow. He died early next morning. But the workhouse continued to offer its bleak hospitality to the unfortunate until the 1930s.

William Cookworthy was another famous Kingsbridge character. He was born in Dodbrooke in 1705, the son of a Quaker weaver. His father died when he was thirteen, leaving his widow with five children. William showed aptitude from early childhood, and soon after his father's death set off to walk to London to seek his fortune. He apprenticed himself to a chemist and in his spare time taught himself Greek, Latin and French, in addition to his scientific and commercial work.

He soon created such an impression among chemists that he was made a partner in a wholesale chemistry firm in 1726. He moved to Plymouth where he lived for the rest of his life, darkened by the death of his wife Sarah in 1745, when he was left with five daughters to raise.

After reading about porcelain production in China, Cookworthy, after twenty years of experiment, discovered kaolinite, a decomposition product of feldspar, in Cornish clay, and made the first "hard paste" porcelain in Britain. He opened factories in Plymouth and Bristol, and his products are now collectors' pieces, beautiful white china domestic and decorative ware, some coloured and gilded. There are birds, animals, human and mythological figures, including an attractive pure white sphinx. The painted decorations include flowers, scrolls and landscapes with classical ruins. There is a fine permanent collection in Plymouth Museum and Art Gallery, and some examples at Kingsbridge, where Cookworthy and Crispin are commemorated in the Cookworthy Museum, the former in the old grammar schoolroom with the headmaster's canopied seat on a dais beneath the arms of Charles II. The original oak panelling covers the walls, incised with generations of schoolboys' initials.

The large proportion of holiday homes and accommodation has altered life in places like Salcombe and Thurlestone, now quite sparsely populated in winter, although I believe that the residents often make up for, in fact make the most of, this in the quality of their lives. But in the outskirts and neighbourhood of Kingsbridge the balance of country life in long-established mellow houses has continued without any very great change, apart from interior modernization. In all the deep and mostly well-wooded peaceful combes around the busy little town are fine houses dating from the sixteenth-, seventeenth- and eighteenth-centuries, settlements going back to medieval and Saxon times, overlooking the estuary or sited alongside streams. On the west are Ilton Castle, now a farm but once a fortified castle; Yarde, which has fine wall-painting; Gerston, home of the Bastard family for twenty generations before they moved to Kitley, where oranges and lemons grew in the nineteenth century, cultivated from seeds or seedlings brought in by the fast fruit clippers; and Abraham Hawkins's Alston, "Athelstan's farm".

On the east side of the estuary, Keynedon Barton near Frogmore has a medieval porch; in the valley that leads up from Bowcombe Bridge, that crosses a creek fed by a stream almost ten miles long, are several old mills, Bearscombe, a fine eighteenth-century house, and, quite invisible from the lane in a thickly wooded side combe, Ranscombe, an exquisite pale-grey gabled Elizabethan mansion with the deep porch typical of Devon houses of the period and a venerable oak front door. Its fine square dovecote stands in the deserted, nettle-filled farmyard, as does the chapel, empty and ivy-covered, whose long history includes having served as a lion-house! And over the hill westward at Buckland-tout-Saints is Buckland House, an eighteenth-century mansion in unusual red brick, now a hotel, also with a dovecote.

But the most important house near Kingsbridge is Bowringsleigh, in the parish of West Alvington. What you see now from the plunging lane on its eastern boundary, is a beautiful Tudor and Jacobean house, silvery-grey among the oaks and beeches of its park, and startlingly large after the modest size of the Kingsbridge town houses. It is a very ancient site, long established even when the Bowrings were living here in 1332. The present owner, Miss Marjorie Ilbert, descends from the family who bought the house in

1696. Various additions up to 1850 were made in accord with the existing style. The oldest surviving part is the chapel, which contains a curiosity in the roodscreen, originally in South Huish church and transferred to Bowringsleigh when the church fell into decay. The seclusion of the sites of South Hams houses, screened by hills and trees, enhances the delight of coming upon them, offered to the eye and yet retaining the mystery of centuries of hidden lives whose story still hovers in the sweet air, tantalizingly felt.

If you continue along the lane that borders the park, over two crossroads and down one of the steepest, narrowest roads in the district, an unusual building appears on the left. This is the gatehouse of Leigh Barton, a perfect example of fourteenth- and fifteenth-century monastic architecture. It is a very narrow two-storeyed building with a fine half-spiral stairway, built of local schist. The gatehouse is not complete nor are the boundary walls. But far from falling into further decay as in so many cases, this is the scene of an exciting rescue operation being undertaken by the Department of the Environment.

When I first visited Leigh in 1981 I was greeted by the three Devon-born experts reconstructing the grange, given a warm welcome and a mug of mid-morning tea, while they explained the project and showed me photographs of the ruined convent before the start of the work. The gatehouse is the entrance to an original Domesday manor that became a cell of Buckfast Abbey. The nearest building across the grass courtyard from the gatehouse is the farmhouse, possibly early medieval and earlier than the L-shaped convent buildings beyond it. In the course of restoration the farmhouse had revealed, under layers of plaster and paper, a fine wooden screen and some decorative plaster, a circular stairwell, stone stairs and a garderobe in an upstairs corner.

The convent itself, traditionally thought to have been a nunnery, is three storeyed, and immensely solid with huge oak beams. Some, severely decayed, have been replaced, others found partly rotten skilfully repaired; the rotten wood is carved away and the rest immersed in Cuprinol. A replacement carved to the exact shape replaces the missing part. Some of the buildings were found in remarkably good shape, in particular the outside staircase leading to the upper storey entrance. A cloister with arched open carved wooden casements continues on after the top of the stairs, a beautiful feature. I had to climb a ladder to see where one of the craftsmen was rebuilding the lath and plaster walls of the top floor. The work was being carried out in the old way with the minimum of modern materials and the maximum of skilled and loving care. This large space was divided into two, perhaps for sleeping quarters.

Protestant Sylvester Gray visited Leigh in 1666 and wrote:

> In one part of the court divers steps lead up to a kind of covered gallery, whence the nuns had access to their chapel, the roof of which was rent and shattered, and the carven images of "wood and stone" to my joy all gone, but the niches that held them remain.

No sign of the niches remains now, but it may be that further research will establish the original arrangement of the convent.

A walk round the outside of the building reveals how solidly it was built. The corners are constructed from L-shaped blocks of schist with beautiful dressing marks, and some of these blocks, although narrow, are over a yard in length on the longer side. The stone came from nearby quarries, and the achievement of carting it, dressing it and fitting the great blocks in the strong walls, demands our admiration.

There was an efficient drainage system. Water entered the kitchen with its two enormous ovens through a hole in the wall from an outside cistern. It was drained out again near ground level and sluiced the garderobe trench before draining away. The gardens, including a herb garden, orchard and fishponds, were off this side of the building.

I was impressed to see that the whole roofless building had been covered with an overlapping roof of new corrugated iron. It will be rehung with the original type of pin-tile, and the mullioned windows replaced. It is inspiring to find, in a remote place that has not greatly changed since Leigh Barton was built, such a dedicated piece of restoration work.

Malborough

The old village of Malborough, a Saxon settlement, lies on the northern edge of the schist plateau; immediately outside it the

Kingsbridge road dips down over red earth. Here a whole network of roads meets, from Salcombe and North· and South Sands they run along the ridges above the valleys, others come from Sewer and Bolberry, and from Inner and Outer Hope on the coast to the west. The superb coastline from Bolt Head to Bolt Tail is in Malborough parish.

From Malborough churchyard can be viewed the full sweep of the South Hams to their northern limit below Dartmoor. On an early spring morning the air is pearly, full of flower scents and birdsong, the sky and sunshine delicate. On an early-dark winter evening the clouds swoop low over the spire that is a landmark from all the hills and gateways for so many miles around, the different cloud-layers travelling in different directions and speeds, spiced with the salt westerly.

When I walked round the village with Jack Yeoman, who has lived in Malborough since the day he was born in 1906, he told me that the slight ridge running northward from the church beside Luckham's Lane was where the women stood watching out for the Parliamentarians while the men manned Burleigh Dolts, a rampart on the next ridge, about a quarter mile away, now disappeared. Malborough, like other districts in the region, was Royalist. Abraham Hawkins gives a description of this "fort" in his book. He says that it fully commands the roads from Modbury and Plymouth to Malborough and Salcombe with its Fort Charles, in an entrenchment "much in the shape of an egg". He assumes that it was thrown up during Charles I's "unhappy wars". He then writes, "Yet it is no less singular than true, that not the smallest traditionary account of it is to be met with in the vicinity. It should seem likely to have been an advance post to oppose the approach of troops from Plymouth towards Fort Charles. . . ." It seems even more singular that I should have been told of the post being manned for defence against the Parliamentarians by Jack Yeoman in the 1980s: as if the memory, now surfaced, had been submerged in Hawkins's day; for he lived at Alston, a stone's throw from Burleigh Dolts.

Luckham's Lane joins the Malborough–Kingsbridge road a hundred yards north of the Malborough crossroads, Townsends Cross; when a tollgate was at the crossroads, earlier called The Turnpike, and the tolls collected from a window of the last house on the right approaching from Kingsbridge, Luckham's Lane was known as The Dodge, for people sneaked up it to avoid paying toll.

We then walked along Upper Town. Other Devon towns and villages have streets named Upper and Lower Town; sometimes Devon farms are named Town, as for instance Cholwich Town. Old English "tun" could mean an enclosure merely; it may be that villages started out as two neighbouring farms or settlements. At the crossroads, two right turns take you past White Hall, an old farmhouse, and down Well Hill on the left. Immediately after another right turn is Shute Well; the ancient spring that feeds it is channelled from higher up on the other side of the road. It has never been known to run dry, even in the drought of 1976. A very old house nearby is called "Chadder's Shute". (Shute or chute means a channel for water.) A lane that runs to the left here is called Quillets. This is a dialect word denoting a strip of land about a furlong in length, and recalls the Saxon methods of strip cultivation. So we were gradually uncovering the signs of Malborough's origins.

Returning up Shute Hill to the right we passed what was one of the two village blacksmiths' shops and the pre-Union workhouse and its garden. Then we walked along Lower Town, first passing Dyer's Cottages. Robert Dyer Esquire lived at the manor farm of Yarde, and on his death in 1730 left a house with a garden and other amenities to the parish for the residence of a schoolmaster, to whom the feoffees of the parish made an allowance of £3 per annum, out of lands given for charitable uses. A feoff, variant of fief, is land or property held in fee for charitable purposes. Feoffees are the officials, now members of the parish or town council, who are invested with the responsibility of administering the feoff. These funds still exist in many villages and towns, and the feoffees discharge their administrative duties as part of their local government work. At Malborough there is a scholarship of £200 that is given to university students as well as other gifts.

The Court is a group of cottages around a wide grass courtyard just off the street. Jack Yeoman was born in one of them. There was one downstairs room, two upstairs, for the family of seven, which Jack assured me was a very happy one. Each cottage had a pigsty; there is still a range of them at one side of the court, long untenanted; and the carpenter's shop he remembers here has gone too. But a rambler rose that grows out of the wall of a stout buttress to one of the cottages was there in his childhood, blooming every year as it still does. The lime in the cob obviously provides it with longevity.

At the turn of the century the cottage rents were ninepence or a shilling a week. In one of the Court cottages the Master of Malborough hounds, another John Yeoman, used to live; the pack was disbanded many years ago. Jack remembers him as a jovial character. After a day's hunting he would go straight to the pub and stay there for the evening. One night his wife's patience ran out. She took his supper along to the pub and dumped it down in front of him: "Here's yer supper John. I'm gwuin to bed!" Another time she put lighted candles all over the house and when John eventually came in and asked her why, she said: "I'm burning, you'm spending!"

Next we walked up Hay Lane, a narrow path that winds between cottages and almost through their gardens but is still a right of way. In a small courtyard here, Hay Court, the workhouse school for the pauper children, was situated in a tiny basement room. There were two other, private, schools in the village, and the county school. The present primary school building is about 120 years old, and the Victorian vicarage, now superseded by the usual smaller modern house, was built about the same time.

Malborough Church, "the Cathedral of the South Hams", is large and filled with light, with high Beer Stone arcades. Although restored to the point of bareness, it does not seem bleak, because of the grace of its fifteenth-century proportions.

Jack Yeoman remembers going to church as a child twice on Sundays and to Sunday school as well. Some of the children had to walk for miles from the outlying farms and hamlets to school and church. Nor was their day ended when school came out. Jack had to fetch water from the well and get a pennyworth of milk in the can. Most people then kept a fattening pig, chickens, and as now grew their vegetables. There were deliveries in those days too, meat and bread came three miles from Salcombe, a fish-cart from South Milton, two miles away, and a hardware wagon came from Kingsbridge. Carts went to Plymouth to fetch fruit and fish and other household goods. Apart from these the village supplied most of its own needs. There were three smithies; most farmers had five or six horses, some more. I can remember the last forge, which was in a huge cavernous shed at the crossroads where Salcombe Road Garage and Spar supermarket now stand, and taking my bay mare Ruby to be shod.

There were two carpenter-wheelwrights, who also made coffins, a butcher's shop and a slaughterhouse. Now Malborough has two supermarkets, a general stores and tobacconist, two garages, two pubs and a large new village hall. There is a sprawl of new development with colourless small houses to the east. But the heart of the ancient village lives on, most of it in Lower Town with one or two lanes that run west out of it; late medieval-style cob thatched cottages with whitewashed walls rounded at the corners in South Hams fashion, little windows with bright potplants on their sills, as nurturing as clotted cream.

Salcombe

The road from Kingsbridge switchbacks over the smooth swell of the rolling farmlands, turning left at Townsend Cross, Malborough. The last two miles swoop eastward along a ridge road to Salcombe. On each side the rounded waves of the fields curve down into valleys, a chequer of red, green and gold, jewelled in spring here and there with the citron of mustard. Soon on the north side you see South Pool creek far below, and on the south a sudden triangle of grey, blue or white-gold is the sea at the end of the North Sands valley. As the outskirts of Salcombe are reached you turn left and with a sensation of landing from the air drop down a steep descent into the village. Ahead is the little symmetrically conical hill above Snapes Point, an individual statement among the school of whalebacks that fill the skylines. Below it the harbour spreads out embroidered with craft of all shapes and colours.

The road winds down Church Hill until at sea-level you are in Fore Street, the narrow thoroughfare that leads through the village and southward along the waterside towards Bolt Head and the open sea. There is an enormous difference in the estuary at high and low tides, in varying kinds of weather. It changes every minute at every stage of time and tide. At a high spring tide "such as moving seems asleep, too full for sound and foam", the water embraces rocks and walls and covers all the sand beaches; at lowest ebb the golden stretches on the east side shine and ripple in sunshine and colour even on the greyest day. Where the sand ends seaweeds and grass lie limply stranded among pebbles and shells where crabs scuttle disorientedly and sink themselves into the ooze up to the eyes.

There is no bridge across the estuary, but a small ferry has made the five-minute crossing from time immemorial. It links up with a part of the coastal path, and the section from Salcombe to Prawle and Start Points can claim to be the most magnificent. There is something unique about the atmosphere of "the other side", as it is called by those on the western shore. It is fresher, sweeter, wilder, more secret yet welcoming. At Lambury Point where the estuary opens out into the sea there are small deep lagoons in the marine platform at low tide that are gardens for a superb selection of sea-weeds whose colours range from mahogany to palest pink. Quite large fish dart from cover to cover, gurnards, not remarkable for beauty but expert at swift manoeuvring, and young, edible black, blue or brown crabs lurk and glide. At the landward end of the pools, where the sea has hollowed smooth beginnings of caves, are little beaches of round white or grey and green-grained pebbles, shining and sparkling, clicking and sucking as the tide recedes. A little further seaward rocky Leek Cove can be reached only by boat or strenuous climbing; it bakes in hot sunshine, and there is an underwater bridge possible for the adventurous to swim through. Between the estuary beaches – Fisherman's Cove, and Millbay with its beautiful valley where in spring kingcups and flags paint splashes of gold along the stream and outsize primroses line the lane in company with sweet-perfumed wild white violets – are delectable rocky coves, and a small sandspit off Sunny Cove offers itself to paddlers and bathers at low tide. In summer the constant procession of yachts and launches provides a continuous pageant, and no matter how bright the day a restful delight for the eye. Salcombe's own tall ships, the Island Cruising Club's Brixham trawler *Provident* and elegant ketch *Hoshi*, arrive and depart at weekends, if the wind is right under their rich chestnut sails, going and coming on their cruises to France, the Channel Islands or Scandinavia.

The sand bar at the harbour entrance lies approximately between Lambury Point and Bar Lodge, "the last house in Salcombe", perched on the wooded cliff on the west side. The position of the bar varies somewhat according to how winter storms combined with fierce tides mould it, although the deep channel for ships of a fair draft remains open on the west side. Good leading lights on shore facilitate night entrance and exit, and the blinking light on hungry Blackstone Rocks reassures all night long until the sun comes up over Portlemouth Down to shine straight into our windows at South Sands. There is a tradition that the bar can be shallow enough to walk across at low spring tide; it is hardly feasible, although I once got out of the boat and waded about, armpit deep, in the middle.

The "moaning" of the bar that Tennyson in his poem begs not to hear is unknown to me; but there is certainly an impressively savage roar from the combers that break all across the bar in storms, such as caused the 1916 lifeboat tragedy when all the crew but two were lost when a breaker turned the open boat over.

The perfect natural harbour of Salcombe was used from the start of seagoing activity. Leland writes in his *Itinerary* that "Saultcombe Haven, sumwhat barrid, and having a Rok at the entering into it, is about vij miles by WSW from Dertmouth; and about half a mile within the mouth of this Haven . . . is Saultcombe, a fishar town". It is still an accurate definition, although fishing and boatbuilding are no longer the great industries they once were here. But the neighbouring channel waters are one of the richest crustacea grounds off Britain; the modern crab industry has reached huge proportions and shows sure signs of overfishing in that the crabs are getting smaller and the lobsters fewer. This is hardly surprising when £4,000 worth of crabs are driven away daily in the summer in refrigerated juggernauts to factories the other side of the country; the trawlers have grown larger and methods more comprehensive. Previously the fishermen went out at dawn and trawled for gurnards, but now bait for the crab and lobster pots comes overland in boxes. Len Fairweather, Salcombe's present-day historian, remembers that once when stocks of bait ran out a party of four fishermen *rowed* the forty miles to Plymouth and back in one day to buy some, a punishing day's pull that is devoured in minutes now by a big power boat.

My mother, a keen fisherman, learned much from the Salcombe experts. Once when talking to a famous character, old Abram Yabsley, she was discussing the art of eating a lobster, and remarked that there was nothing worth having in the legs. "Oo, do 'ee throw they out?" asked Abram, shocked. "I picks they up and sucks they!" After that we always did so, and it is true that they are full of juicy shreds of meat.

We used to go fishing with Jack Cook in the sturdy white clinker-built motor-boat *Girl Pat*, built in Salcombe. The Cook family have lived in Salcombe for centuries, boatbuilders and fishermen, who began to augment their income by taking out visitors when Salcombe became popular as a holiday resort. Old Harry Cook, Jack's uncle, was said to live up to his name; he had bright twinkling sailor's blue eyes and an endless fund of tales. Jack was the best kind of uncle to us. His cheery whistle, *Half a pound of pork and dripping*, would bring us running down to the South Sands jetty for a morning's fishing followed by picnics on the rocks at Starehole Bay or up one of the estuary creeks if it was rough. He taught me to row when I was ten, letting me loose to "catch crabs" in the blunt little clinker-built dinghy called by my name; he kept us in order by hanging us upside down over the side till our hair was dunked in the sea, or putting big slithering sand-eels down our backs. He sang and whistled his favourite tunes – not folksongs, but *Little Sir Echo* and *South of the Border*. He was infinitely patient and generous of his lore and his time, an expert weather forecaster: "In with your lines, fog's coming up," when to our eyes the sky was clear, or "It'll only be a liddle scat. There, turned out nice again, init?" He knew when the mackerel were coming, where to fish for the fine hard-to-catch bass, where to drop lobster pots, the best area for deep-sea trawling, when the net would come up filled with treasure: clown-faced skate with long tails, flounders, occasionally a conger-eel that could bark like a dog and snap off a finger with ease, and spiny little sea-urchins. Jack's keen blue eyes and brown arms are unforgettable, his hands testing the lines, hauling pots, cleaning fish over the stern with an attendant wake of wheeling screaming gulls. The only thing he was absolutely unshakeable about when we wanted to stay out was to be home at five. He and his wife Nellie were devoted; when Nellie died in 1982 Jack's life ended too. He pined and was gone in three months; it was a death difficult to comprehend, so vital had he been.

Jack's sons Leslie and Terry have followed him and are fishermen too, crabbing in their thirty-four-foot boat with two hundred pots. They usually set them about three miles out off Prawle Point. The biggest Salcombe boats go out with five hundred pots to the strip midway between the two east- and westbound traffic lanes in the Channel. The pots are hauled up now mechanically with the modern sleigh method – two spring-loaded circular plates rotating together between which the pot wire runs. It is a dangerous system, recently one man lost an arm and several have had fingers severed. The weather does seem to grow more unpredictable and sometimes in winter the crabbers can get out only once or twice a week. You can hear their boats' powerful motors on their way out in the small hours, returning late next day. It is still quite a hard life. But the financial rewards are good; and when seagoing is impossible in winter there is still some trawling for scallops, the local "oysters", in the harbour.

Side by side with the fishing industry grew the trades of piracy and smuggling. Chaucer's portrait of a Shipman was a true likeness, filching wine from under the sleeping Bordeaux chapman's nose and taking no keep of "nyce conscience". Salcombe harbour and the many hidden wooded inlets of the creeks conveniently sheltered gentlemen who sailed out to plunder passing ships or smuggle in contraband. In 1607 the County justices complained to the government about the "sundry dissolute seafaring men" who sometimes raided the town two hundred strong, threatening to burn it down if their demands were not met. They stole sheep and sometimes the fishermen's boats, and it was said, somewhat ungrammatically, that they "murdered each other, and buried them in the sands by night". In 1625 Sir William Courtenay's castellated mansion, Ilton Castle, was raided by pirates who took much of his plate and household goods.

Medieval Salcombe seems to have been a less important place than East Portlemouth opposite, perhaps because Portlemouth was built higher up the steep hillside and so was less accessible to incursions. Its name, recorded in Domesday as belonging to Judhel, Baron of Totnes, carries more weight; and it was on the shores below Portlemouth village that the first ships known to have been supplied from this haven were built. Portlemouth sent five ships and ninety-six men to join the fleet that transported the ten thousand English longbowmen to victory for Edward III at the Battle of Crécy in 1346. Two hundred years later Salcombe is mentioned as a supplier of ships, having now followed Portlemouth's example, and in 1588 the towns and villages around the haven shores fitted out sixteen vessels to join the defence against the Armada.

For the century and a half after the defeat of the Armada little shipbuilding was carried out at Salcombe, apart from fishing craft, but towards the end of the eighteenth century trade increased rapidly and Salcombe began to expand the industry which became its chief occupation. Shipyards grew up along the present harbour frontage, fairly haphazard constructions that during the last decades have all disappeared. Supplementary trades began, shipsmiths, spar- and blockmakers, sailmakers and chandlers. There was ropemaking at Kingsbridge from 1783, the Ropemark marks the site at the western head of the estuary. It supplied the Salcombe shipyards, the Newfoundland and Labrador fisheries and the shipyard established at Kingsbridge in 1837, the year of Victoria's accession.

1864 marked the height of the Salcombe/Kingsbridge shipbuilding and trading prosperity. In that year there were ninety-eight foreign-going ships and an equal number of coasting and harbour vessels. The fruit clippers were the local speciality, wooden barques, brigantines, brigs and schooners, from 100 to 550 tons. Oak for their planks came from trees around the estuary, hewn and transported by rowboat "tugs" or hauled through the narrow miry lanes on wagons, to be hand-sawn at the yards. The clippers, small fast tall ships, were built to bring perishable cargoes of oranges, pineapples and coconuts as fast as possible from the Azores, the Mediterranean and the West Indies; their skilful skippers could get them right up to London Bridge to catch the Covent Garden market under their own sail, a pineapple jammed on the boom as an advertising figurehead. But these mariners, like some of their yacht-racing successors, often paid the price of speed records. Many families in Salcombe and Kingsbridge mourned drowned relatives lost in foreign waters without trace.

Ships came to Salcombe laden with exotic cargoes: rum, spices, cocoa, coffee, tobacco, oils, wines, silks, from the West Indies and the Americas. Salcombe ships visited the ports of the world, and the sailors had their own shanty that began:

> A lofty ship from Salcombe came,
> Blow high, blow low, and so wailed we . . .

By the end of the nineteenth century two hundred three-masters could be seen in the harbour together, sheltering from storms. The narrow length of Fore Street runs close to the waterside, and it could happen that an extra long bowsprit would invade a house on the far side of the street through a bedroom window, which must have been draughty for the occupants when a north-easterly was blowing.

The sea captains of Salcombe grew wealthy. They built themselves villas in solid Victorian style along the elegant curve of Devon Road, and their wives furnished them with the exotic gifts their men brought home. Paintings of the clippers, many of which can be seen at Overbecks Museum, hung on their walls.

But by the beginning of World War One only five trading vessels were registered in the local port book and all of those were owned outside the district. There was little shipbuilding from then on, apart from wooden fishing boats and dinghies, Edgar Cove's fine whalers for the Navy, and the Salcombe Yawl, which had been developed from the early small wooden crabbing boats. It is Bermudan-rigged with a foresail and a larger mainsail, and a mizzen mast and sail at the stern. When they were hauling their pots the crabbers could lower the mainsail, and the foresail and mizzen would hold the boat's directional stability in a choppy sea. This feature, and the sturdy design of the sixteen-foot clinker-built craft, ensured the success of the boat. The yawls' three different-sized white wings above its solid yet graceful hull fit perfectly in its habitat, in some mysterious way defining it as integral to Salcombe. No other boat looks so much a native of the place.

The crab fishermen began to race their yawls in the nineteenth century. Although all built to the same basic design there could be variations, and during the 1930s when visitors and non-fishermen began to buy the boats for racing and pleasure, specifications for the Salcombe yawl were drawn up for a restricted class. Since then 114 boats have been built, the majority in Salcombe by Jim Stone at his boatyard in the small bay at Goodshelter. The specifications require the hull, decks, seats and masts to be made of wood and not plastic, carrying on the old tradition.

Jim Stone is now eighty-one years old, a sprightly man who on an afternoon in November 1982 was busy gluing on the foredeck of Yawl No. 114 – its registration neatly chiselled into the wooden deck. Jim tells the history of the yard: when his father, who began his working life as a crab-pot maker and was, says Jim, "the best friend, the best neighbour, the best adviser, the best man I have ever known", heard that a farmer friend had bought all the land and buildings at Waterhead, Mr Stone asked to buy a couple of the farm sheds, and that was the beginning of the boatyard. Jim, born in 1902, built his first yawl when he was sixteen, and in the same year won the regatta sailing race in his own new boat. His son Alex, who with his wife lives and works with Jim, started the race in that crabbing yawl when he was nine. Jim still uses the box of tools his father bought for him when he began work; it cost just £8. He has lived and worked at home all his life, apart from a spell during World War Two when he narrowly escaped death by bombing while working as a shipwright for the Navy at Devonport; he has seen great changes, although not in his own peaceful corner, and some tragedies – he witnessed the lifeboat disaster in 1916, with the loss of men who were all his friends. They had been called out to a distressed ship which in fact managed to survive without their help, and were on their way back to harbour. They were accustomed to lower their sails and row over the bar, and it was as they turned up into the wind to let down the sails that a mighty wave hit the lifeboat and overturned it.

Salcombe's maritime history is commemorated in the Maritime Museum, mounted in a loft above an old boathouse on Island Quay, with a fisherman's cottage interior, shipwrights' tools and much more.

There is little older architecture left in the town, the best houses are the Victorian sea-captains' homes. But at Lower Batson, a hundred yards around the creekside past the boat-park at the north-west corner of the town, is a group of ancient cottages at the head of Batson Creek. Below Snapes Point on the north side of this creek lies Snapes Manor, "a neat snug box". At Upper Batson, on a corkscrew hill that joins the main Salcombe–Malborough road, is the former manor house, now Batson Hall Farm. The house has been restored, but on the roadside are two ruined ivy-covered buildings said to have been a prison where captives were chained to await trial by Judge Jeffreys, whose seventeenth-century reign of terror extended even to this remote spot. Happier memories of Batson are of cider wassailing. The orchards of this sheltered valley claimed to be renowned throughout the kingdom, and on the eve of Epiphany the farmer and his men would go out to his orchard, taking with them a pitcher of cider and loaded guns. At the foot of one of the most productive trees they repeated this age-old toast three times:

> Here's to thee
> Old apple tree,
> Whence thou may'st bud,
> And whence thou may'st blow,
> And whence thou may'st bear
> Apples enow;
> Hats full!
> Caps full!
> Bushel bushel sacks full!
> And my pockets full too!
> Huzza!

After the third toast the guns were shot off, and when the pitcher was empty the men returned to the house, to find the doors locked against them, however hard the weather. The women inside refused to let them in before one had guessed what was roasting on the spit. It was the custom to choose something unusual to keep the men guessing.

There were numerous feasts and ceremonies throughout the year; something of "nut-brown mirth and russet wit" lives on among Devonians, and the vernacular is still spoken. Devonshire is a language rather than a dialect, with its special words and phrases and soft enunciation. Pat Pratt, the Salcombe postmistress, is addressed as "maid" by some of the older citizens: "When you'm dead, maid, there'll be no one left," they say. Pat has a fund of stories, and remembers the jollity when her grandmother held court in a small cottage at Holset near Portlemouth, where she lived with her farmworker husband and eleven children. They would sit around a scrubbed table on trestles feasting on dockyardie, a dish originating from Plymouth, made of fat pork, onion, potato and turnips, followed by home-made bread, strawberry jam and a huge bowl of golden crusty clotted cream in the middle of the table. In the outhouse were Grandmother Baskerville's casks of home-brewed stout, where Pat was once discovered as a toddler considerably under its influence.

No church was built at Salcombe in the early Middle Ages. The parish church was at Malborough, two Devonshire miles inland. (A Devonshire mile by tradition measures at least three normal ones!) Without a church and priest the bold pirates had everything their own way. Eventually the God-fearing people of Salcombe decided to combat piracy with piety and raised funds for the building of a Chapel of Ease to enable them to worship on their home ground. It was erected in 1399 and licensed in 1401. But burials were still carried out at Malborough and it was not until 1841, when the prosperity of the shipyards had doubled the population of Salcombe, that a new church was built and consecrated in 1844. An undisguised thirteenth-century reproduction, its position on a rise overlooking the harbour makes it a pleasant landmark and its clock chimes over the water with a homely ring.

A mile along the scenic cliff road, on the spur flanking North Sands bay, stands the ruin of Salcombe Castle, Fort Charles. The castle, whose romantic remains stand on the marine platform at the northern point of North Sands bay, lashed by seas breaking from the Bar, is reputed to have been built by Henry VIII on an older site. When the Parliamentarians were advancing towards South Devon, Royalist Sir Edmund Fortescue of Fallapit, near Kingsbridge, offered and was commissioned to refortify and equip the castle in 1645. It won renown the following year by being the last stronghold in Devon to hold out against the Parliamentarians. It was well equipped, Sir Edmund spent £1,355. 18s. 9d. on the building and £1,031. 19s. 9d. on "timber, ordnance, powder, shot, muskets, swords, and various warlike articles". His provisions for the force of sixty-six men and two laundresses included ten hogsheads of punch, one tun of March Beer, ten tuns of cider, twenty-two hogsheads of beef and pork and much more.

The siege when it came lasted from January to May 1646, when the castle surrendered. The besieged forces were permitted to return to their homes and Sir Edmund was even allowed to march his troop to Fallapit with drums beating and colours flying.

North Sands valley and its branches run towards Malborough, traversed by one of the deepest, roughest and oldest lanes in the district. As it winds upward it gets darker where the hazel and alder

Salcombe, c. 1920

Salcombe, North Sands Bay

St Werburgh's Church, Wembury

Buckland Abbey

Drake on Plymouth Hoe

View from the Citadel, Plymouth

Royal Albert Bridge, Plymouth

hedge-trees clasp branches above its green and red tunnel, worn by centuries of erosion to a rocky base. After heavy rain the banks slip more tons of red sticky soil to be worn down in their own time.

On the hilly spur dividing North from South Sands stands the principal house of Salcombe, The Moult. Since it was built in 1764 by John Hawkins as "a mere pleasure box", it has had a succession of owners and tenants. In 1795 Samuel Strode, the owner then, bequeathed it to his widow, "the once beautiful and elegant Miss Grace Caulfield", as Abraham Hawkins somewhat ambiguously describes her, saying that ". . . while she passed the brumal season in town, The Moult was her favourite abode on the return of Flora's adscititious graces and Pomona's delightful bounties . . ." During part of the nineteenth century the house was occupied by James Anthony Froude, the historian. He was a Devonian, born at Dartington. In a letter from The Moult about 1881 he wrote: "It is near midnight. I have just come in from the terrace. The moon is full over the sea, which is glittering as if it was molten gold. The rocks and promontories stand out clear and ghostlike. There is not a breath to rustle the leaves or to stir the painted wash upon the shore." Froude's American friend Bret Harte also enthused over The Moult and its position when he was on a visit; it is hard not to be effusive here.

Salcombe people like to maintain that Tennyson wrote the poem *Crossing the Bar* after visiting Froude at The Moult in 1889, but this cannot be certainly proved, although Tennyson, frail after serious illness the previous year, did stay in Salcombe harbour in the yacht *Sunbeam*. His son Hallam said that the poem was written in October 1889 while crossing the Solent as they sailed from Aldworth to Farringford. But it may well be that the departure from Salcombe stayed in the poet's memory to inspire the poem.

Part of the steep northern side of South Sands valley, that belonged to the Earl of Devonshire, was sold off in building plots at the turn of this century, as similarly other parts of Salcombe had been. Before then there were only The Moult, the lifeboat house and a couple of cottages in this area, until Captain Trinick built Bolt Head Hotel of wood "in the Norwegian style". Its exterior is relatively unchanged although enlarged.

Our house, built in 1906, stands on a platform made by blasting out some of the solid schist of the hillside; it is surrounded by trees, indigenous and planted, Scots pine, bay, blue pine, yew, cupressus, oak, beech and pittosporum. Hydrangeas, fuchsias and camellias flourish, and wild strawberries take over from the grass on the banks. Along the lane behind the house sloes pearl their bushes with their hard, dark-blue berries silvered with efflorescent bloom, and blackberries offer their never-failing crop from August onwards. Many creatures share our woodland: scolding squirrel families resent human presence, and sometimes bump crossly against the verandah windows; slow-worms live in the garden walls and toads keep to their regular routine evening walks. We have bats nesting in the roof, and visiting brown or green crickets come to stay in the house in summer, although they do not take up hearthside residence. Every summer the space in front of the house between the trees is the scene of several great golden dragonflies' aerobatics; we also enjoy the voices of jays and green woodpeckers and the company of at least two house-robins, as well as chaffinches, tits, treecreepers, warblers, stock-doves, wood pigeons, wrens and firecrests. Sometimes after blizzards flocks of stranded redstarts appear, blown off course and not always able to survive. Above us is an old-established rookery, undislodgeable despite some neighbours' attempts at shooting the birds out. Their normal discourse sometimes rises to a crescendo at the approach of a marauding kestrel eyeing their nests, and they mob the wheeling predator until it makes off.

Autumn is the star season. The Milky Way is particularly clear here, Orion stands in all his strength, and Venus is supremely bright. The moon makes a path to infinity over the sea, its million moving glints travelling over the black or ultramarine waters, and the shape of the cliffs is darkness itself behind them. Occasionally one can see a shooting star; and down to earth the miniature green star of a glow-worm against a wall.

Winter can come in a sudden stormy violence, and then ebb again into balmy days of pale sunshine warm enough to sit out in. In early December 1981 there was a day of malevolently freakish fury; from 10 a.m. to 5 p.m. the dark livid sky threw down sleet and snow out of an easterly stormforce gale. The noise of sea and tormented trees was astounding; the whole sea boiled white all day. At five it suddenly calmed, and people crept out from their houses, where they had boiled tea-water over open fires or by calor gas as there had been a power failure, to look at the crashing breakers. The waves had sent tons of sand over the walls at North and South Sands, the gale had torn boats from their moorings and flung them on rocks in the harbour, trees had been uprooted over a wide area. But despite the ferocity it had been exhilarating.

The first Salcombe lifeboat station was established at South Sands in 1869; before then the only people who went to the rescue of sailors in distress were the coastguards. The beautiful red granite lifeboat house has echoes of Dutch building style; it was presented to the Royal National Lifeboat Institution by Richard Durant of Sharpham near Totnes, as a plaque with an inscription and his coat of arms records. Now the stout wooden slipway is covered in summer with windsurfing boards and sunbathers, and the sand with people and small boats of all kinds. The motor ferry from Salcombe plies through the day, landing its passengers on to an old wartime amphibious craft that chugs slowly to keep pace with the changing state of the tide.

An ancient custom that, like frequented paths, had become a right, was operated from South Sands. Farmers loaded seaweed and sand on to donkeys that plodded up the path through Tor Woods on the south side of the valley to fertilize the fields at the top.

Up the hill and past Splat Cove below Bolt Head Hotel brings you to the start of the Round Walk, the road ends finally at the National Trust car park next to Overbecks Gardens and Museum, the former home of Dr Otto Overbeck, who left his house, natural history collections and grounds to the National Trust on his death in 1937. The magnificent gardens are renowned for the gigantic old waxy cream and rose magnolia trees that are a breathtaking sight when their chalices open in late March and April, and for many rare plants and shrubs, including palms, myrtle, eucalyptus and camphor. Another rarity in English gardens is the American aloe (*Agave amaryllis*) which occasionally appears at Salcombe. Like the citrus trees, the aloe was probably introduced by a sea captain. In 1774 one grew to the huge proportions of twenty-eight feet high, including its flower head, and recently another aloe grew from some long-hidden seed and flowered in the garden of a house above Salcombe Castle, to the astonishment of the owners.

The views from Overbecks Gardens over the sea to Prawle Point and down the estuary to Salcombe match those from the top of

Capri; and the wild flowers on the cliffs and valley sides further along bid fair to outmeasure the garden beauties in their colourful variety of form and native charm. A stream runs down the valley above Starehole Bay just east of Bolt Head, and in one place about half a mile up it, there is a bridge across. In the marshy area of the stream here a wild garden of water-loving plants flourishes in July: wild angelica with its purple stems and round ball of creamy florets, fragrant water-mint, the furry-leaved great willow herb and hemp agrimony tower over tormentil and creeping cinquefoil. A little higher on drier soil the minute blue stars of sheepbit grow near wild thyme, mint, lousewort and ragwort, toadflax and fleabane, and on top of the cliffs black knapweed contrasts with the soft blue scabious against the background of wind-trimmed gorse and creeping honeysuckle. A lark soars from under your feet and you share in its exultant liberation.

CAVE

Sea has called off the watchdogs
left the way in unguarded
made peace with the sun
for a day; waves us
gently in through the dark
entrance under the red sheer
of cliff. The boy rows
quietly until oars scrape
on rock and one must out
from rowlock, push on rock
and look, between old drips
that bell the greenblack waterfloor
colours amaze: rose to brown,
black to adamantine, indigo,
under and over shining into eyes
adjusting to the glim. Light comes
windowed from a jag of height.

Something is understood; a place given
like a name. To call it,
passing next year with wind following,
we will say, "There's that cave
we went in," remembering
the dark calm and the light blaze
coming out, forgetting
we are in it always now.

Chapter Eight

SOUTHERN SEASCAPE

WE HAVE MADE the coast of South Devon into a paradox. For the coastline and its hinterland comprise an area of natural beauty that is in places wild and little known, even difficult of access; yet also two areas of conurbation formed out of once separate villages: the huge tourist-oriented county borough of Torbay, and the city of Plymouth, also a county borough. All are contained in the relatively small region described in this book, covering about 600 square miles.

The whole region presents strong contrasts: between romantic village and wild moorland, mild summer and savage blizzard, modern architecture, as in Plymouth's new Theatre Royal, and the ruins of ancient castles and houses. It is a range that with the mysterious quality of prehistoric monuments, and the land's secret places, is inexhaustible. But in a maritime county the sea is the greatest natural influence on human history, with the coast providing ports of embarkation and return for every kind of voyage: of discoveries by the Hawkins family of Plymouth, Drake and Raleigh, the Gilberts and many more. Of battle and piracy – the indented coastline has aided our own sailors, raiders, smugglers, privateers and excisemen. The harbours still shelter the intrepid global sailors of this century, fishermen and naval ships.

A voyage along the coast from Exmouth to Plymouth is an experience that offers most kinds of visual delight as well as a sense of adventure. The beautiful coastline varies as the changing geological strata meet the sea. Near both ends of the section, at Torquay and Plymouth, the limestone cliffs are silvery or grey and have revealed priceless repositories of prehistoric treasures, most importantly at Kent's Cavern, Torquay, and at Orestone Cave, Plymouth. The crimson new red sandstone of the cliffs around Dawlish and Teignmouth contrasts with the golden sandspits of Exmouth and Dawlish; the broad band of Dartmouth slates gives the shining vertical slabs of cliff near Blackpool Sands and between the Erme and Yealm as well as quieter variations of colour. The schists of the southernmost points provide the formidable grandeur from Start to Bolt Tail; and the river mouths invite with offers of safe tree-sheltered anchorage after struggle with the sea, and the sensation of all sailors returning to dry land from their own element: relief, pleasurable anticipation of food, drink and other comforts, but at the same time the slight heaviness of coming back to earth.

Sailing from east to west, after Exmouth the coast takes a straight line past Dawlish with its memories of such discursive guests as Jane Austen and Charles Dickens, its long beach and promenade and the series of tunnels excavated through the red cliffs that makes travelling on Brunel's railway line from Exeter to Newton Abbot a series of brief revelations of seascape, cliff and beach.

At Teignmouth the town is not greatly changed since the time when Keats and Fanny Burney stayed there, Keats at a house in the Strand for a couple of months in 1818, from March to May, looking after his brother Tom in the vain hope that the mild climate would help him to fight off the consumption that Keats himself probably contracted then. He had mixed feelings about Devon, finding the weather abominable (it was an especially wet spring), but the primroses fine, although "the Primroses are out, but then you are in". However, he managed to enjoy some good walks when the sun deigned to appear, and explored the shore and the neighbourhood:

> For there's Bishop's teign
> And King's Teign
> And Coom at the clear teign head.
> Where close by the Stream
> You may have your cream
> All spread upon barley bread.

On the opposite, west side of the river mouth Shaldon, connected to Teignmouth by a road bridge, has delightful Georgian houses below the Ness, and a sharply-rising bright red sandstone head-land. Risdon reports an invasion of the Danes here in 970.

> In memory whereof, the clift exceeding red,
> Doth seem thereat again full fresh to bleed,

for the beach below, and the spit forming the harbour entrance, are coloured pink by the red sandstone breccias. This part of the coast, from Branscombe near Seaton round to Torquay, is formed of the reddest rock strata, that runs inland to Exeter.

The section of coast between The Ness at Teignmouth and Hope's Nose at Torquay forms the slight curve of Babbacombe Bay, whose steep cliffs are indented with numerous sandy coves. Limestone Hope's Nose houses an enormous noisy colony of kittiwakes, as if announcing the arrival of craft to Torquay Harbour two miles further around the coast, from here to Berry Head almost totally covered by the buildings of Torbay.

This region is an illustrated history of the English seaside holiday, well established by the nineteenth century. It came into being when the development of the Industrial Revolution brought wealth and leisure to the middle classes. The demand for "watering places" is marked in the house-building of the seaside towns. At the beginning of the nineteenth century there was no holiday industry at Torquay. It developed chiefly because of its sheltered site, and good climate, found beneficial for invalids, and also because during the Napoleonic Wars the fleet often used Torbay as a safe anchorage, and officers' wives stayed in the small village of Tor Quay, named after the quay built in the medieval period by the monks of Torre Abbey. From then on, what had originated as three small settlements that became parishes, Tor Mohun, St Marychurch and Cockington, grew into the thriving Victorian resort with its terraced houses, wide boulevards, palm-shaded parks, pier and yacht harbour. In this century it has sprawled in every direction until it is virtually linked up with Newton Abbot to the north-west and completely with Paignton to the west.

But the town itself retains elegance. It has been grandiloquently likened to Rome, owing to its site on eight rather than seven hills, which provide constantly changing viewpoints and perspectives. The ruined Abbey with its huge medieval barn and the eighteenth-century mansion built near it are in the spacious Abbey Gardens near the sea in the centre of the easternmost corner of the bay.

Chiefly responsible for the development of Torquay as a fashionable resort were several generations of the Palk family of

Haldon, Dunchideock, who employed architects early in the nineteenth century to create the terraces, crescents and parades of classically graceful, white stuccoed houses, large-windowed to the sea views, towered, pilastered, columned and pedimented, and set along wide roadways in large gardens that remain, covering over half the area of the town, and that in many places still give the impression of an exotic landscape with villas.

Beneath the surface beauties of Torquay, Kent's Cavern is an immense network of underground caves formed by the erosion of the limestone outcrop of the hillside below Wellswood a mile north-west of the harbour. The first scientific exploration of the caves was made during 1859–60 by the Revd W. MacEnery, Dean W. Buckland and William Pengelly. The finds of palaeolithic implements beside the bones of prehistoric animals in the successive layers of the cave floor deposits put paid to the old belief that man was not as old as the pleistocene era. Palaeolithic man had sheltered in the cave as had cave hyaenas, mammoths, bears, rhinoceroses, lions, sabre-toothed tigers, bison, reindeer, elks and horses. One of the finest features of the cave is the beautiful shading of green and pink of the limestone stalactites and stalagmites.

I had always regarded the resort of Paignton as an uninteresting suburb of Torquay until I began to look at it closely instead of merely taking children to the excellent zoo. In one day I visited two houses that present an extreme contrast. The original, probably Saxon, village, was settled half a mile inland; the bishops of Exeter discovered the fertility of the soil here and built a palace near the church of which a few remnants exist. The fine red sandstone church is the centre of the old town, with a few other old buildings. Near it, Kirkham House is cared for by the Department of the Environment. It is of about late fourteenth-century date and a fine medieval town house, also in the deep red local stone. Carefully restored, it is welcoming, solid and gracious. It is also in impeccable taste: great timbers in beams, doors and roof, and the screens passage, are superbly carved and moulded. There were stone wash basins in the parlour and hall, two staircases, the usual offices in the form of garderobes; the floors are of pitched pebbles and the roof slate, and there was an adjoining kitchen and garden. From one window you can just see the church clock, which must have been useful for the occupants of the house.

After Kirkham House I went on to see Oldway Mansion, not far
to the east. The contrast was ludicrous. After the soft stone, dark
wood and irregular rounded cobbles, here shines in brilliant white
what its creator called "The Wigwam". He was Isaac Merritt
Singer, founder of the Singer Sewing Machine Company, who
bought the Fernham estate here in 1871 and employed a local
architect to design his mansion and a circular "Riding and
Exercising Pavilion". The house was to resemble a huge French
villa. Unfortunately for Mr Singer it was not finished until after his
death in 1875. From 1904–7 one of his sons made considerable
alterations to make the house mirror the style of Versailles, with a
long colonnade with nine Ionic columns. It is Paignton's equivalent
of Rome's "Wedding Cake". There are over one hundred rooms,
but it is the hall and staircase that are most amazing in their florid
ornamentation. The grand staircase and gallery have floor and walls
of multi-coloured marble, the staircase is marble with balusters of
bronze, all around the gallery are huge marble pillars with gilded
capitals and volutes supporting an elaborate cornice; the vaulted
ceiling is covered with a densely detailed medley of Italianate
painting in which gold predominates. Two vast brass figures sit in
niches.

Paignton itself can offer its own natural chamber of costly stones,
infinitely more attractive to me than Oldway: the Crystal Cave in
Waterside Cove, a cave whose sides are almost entirely formed of
calcite. On the rocks outside is a network of thick calcite veins, but
the interior of the cave glitters and shines with crystals. It is to be
hoped that mineral hunters with picks and hammers will leave it in
peace, for it has already suffered much damage. In Waterside Cove
the Devonian slates have been moulded into beautiful purple
pebbles and fragments, and the red mudstones with pyrites in them
also contain minute fossils of several species.

The next port of call is Brixham, at the western end of Torbay,
opposite Torquay. Its small bay did not provide a sheltered natural
harbour like the river estuaries, and sea walls were built towards the
end of the eighteenth century and enlarged from time to time until
1974. The famous trawler fishing industry started at about the same
time as the harbour took shape. For long Brixham was one of the
most important fishing ports in the country and its trawlermen in

their fine sturdy ships sometimes circumnavigated Britain in their search for fish. Life for the men at sea and their families at home, netmaking and knitting, in sparse comfort in small houses built on the steep slopes above the little port, was grimly tough but seasoned with Devonian humour and courage. The sailing trawlers continued to work until the start of World War Two. After a lull the industry has revived with power trawlers; now it is almost impossible for visiting craft to find anchorage in the crowded little harbour, where a replica of the *Golden Hind* towers brightly painted above the fishing boats. Although most of the architecture of the town is dull late nineteenth- and twentieth-century, there are some older buildings of character near the quays, and the town as a whole, covering the hillsides, is attractive, although not to be compared with Topsham or Kingsbridge.

Brixham Museum is run on a voluntary basis by a self-styled group of amateurs. It moved in 1977 to its present premises in the old police station at Bolton Cross. Among the chief exhibits are items commemorating the maritime history of the town and its shipbuilding, in the form of workshops and rooms in fishermen's houses, with a wealth of varied artefacts. The chief archaeological treasure is a crouched skeleton from 1200 BC, found in the district.

In 1970 the flat area on top of Berry Head, the high limestone headland on the promontory west of Brixham, was bought from the trustees of the family of the Revd H. F. Lyte, first incumbent of Lower Brixham Church from 1824 onwards. He lived at Berry Head House, where he wrote the hymn *Abide With Me*. The purchasers, the County Borough of Torquay, opened Berry Head as a country park in 1970, European Conservation Year.

I was once there at the end of December on a stormy day. Above me purplish blue and dove grey swelling rainclouds raced eastward with small gaps of blue sky between them, and here and there hazy sunlight fell on parts of Torquay, lighting up the white houses. There were numerous ships sheltering in Torbay as they have done for a thousand years, after a night of gale, thunder, lightning and torrential rain. A kestrel hovered above the cliff edge absolutely stationary even in the strong wind. There were only a few cars in the discreetly bank-shielded park in a dip below the remains of the fort. This is in two sections, one near the point on the site of an ancient earthwork, one of the Iron Age coastal forts, the inner, and larger, to the south-west but still near the cliff. It covers a large area, with a moat and sturdy defensive outer wall, built in 1802–3 at the time of the Napoleonic invasion scare. It is a stunning viewpoint, the cliff is dizzily high here, and a good site for the small lighthouse set back from the edge.

On the cliff top above the slight bay west of the point a notice prohibits cliff-climbing between 15 May and 15 July. Here is a breeding colony of auks: guillemot, razorbill and fulmar. It's remarkable that these birds, relatively rare in the south, can breed, and wild animals thrive, so close to a huge built-up area. As I walked inside the larger fort area, a hare ran across from one gorse patch to another in one direction, and a weasel in the other; he was a handsome fellow who stopped and sat up when he reached his gorse patch and stared at me, showing his white shirt front.

From Sharkham Point, further west, the limestone gives way to slates and grits again, still high and affording glorious views from above and impressive heights from the sea, until the mouth of the Dart.

From Dartmouth, sailing west past the rocks called The Dancing Beggars, you come to the small wood-lined cove, Blackpool Sands, an idyllic place with a bloody history. An attack by invading Bretons in 1400 was repulsed by the defenders of Dartmouth who slaughtered the Frenchmen. The crowds of summer visitors to the bay seem unaffected by the memory, but locals do not like the atmosphere here.

On the cliff top about a mile west of Blackpool Sands, traversed by the coastal road, is the village of Strete. Here Cordelia and Edward Baskerville, cousins of my Salcombe friend Pat Pratt, live at Manor Farm, a medieval manor. From outside, the house looks unexceptional now, a large long cottage, tiled, with modern windows, at right angles to a side street. But while making alterations with the aid of their builder son-in-law Colin Gill they uncovered some exciting details, including a deep fireplace with ovens at the side in the old kitchen. A more unusual find came when they were removing some old plaster from an upstairs bedroom fireplace with a pick, and realized just in time that there was a design beneath the top layers. It proved to be sgraffito decoration similar to that, for example, in late medieval merchants' houses in Plymouth. There is also a "smoke room" in the very centre of the house. This is a conical shaped space with walls of rough schist rising to a pointed ceiling that would originally have had a hole to let the smoke escape. It must have been used for smoking meat or fish, but is a rare feature to have survived. Freshly white-painted, and not soot-layered as it must have been, it is attractive now. The old house possesses any number of strange nooks and protuberances, demonstrating many alterations throughout the centuries.

A quarter of a mile or so west of Strete the high coastal road dips, turns a hairpin bend, and descends to sea level to run beside the flat one-and-a-half-mile long stretch of shingle barrier beach, oddly called Slapton Sands. This, "The Line", is the most interesting geomorphological phenomenon in South Devon. On the north, landward, side of the road is Slapton Ley Nature Reserve. There are two leys, the Lower Ley, an open freshwater lake with a thick reed fringe, and the Higher Ley, a lake now silted up with marsh and vegetation. It is a vitally important plant and animal habitat.

Geologists now consider the shingle banks to have stabilized about 3000 years ago and the lakes to be about 1000 years old. Before then the two streams that flow into them, the Gara and the Start, would have run out into the sea, making channels for themselves even after the shingle bar started to form. It is interesting to observe that in his map of Devon from 1575, Saxton shows the Gara and the Start thus, and the Gara as having quite a wide estuary for some distance inland. He gives no indication of the barrier; but he is not always accurate over details, for all the beauty of his maps, and may not have been to Slapton himself to verify facts. Leland, who did go everywhere that he describes in his *Itinerary*, particularly mentions the Slapton barrier, and the freshwater lake with plentiful fish.

One of the best views of The Line and the Leys is from the west, on the sudden height of the cliff top at Torcross. The long chesil stretches its slightly curved length to Strete with an exhilarating impression of strength and simplicity. The southward-bounding sea is smilingly wrinkled in summer, although the shingle beach shelves downward abruptly, but in winter the full force of a south-westerly gale sent twenty-foot breakers crashing on to the houses along the shore in 1978, damaging several. Now there are new sea defences made, with a concrete wall and huge blocks of pink and grey slate. But the impression of simplicity is entirely false where plant and animal life is concerned. The shingle ridge hosts different plants on the shoreward and the landward sides, the shores of the Leys across the road vary again, and the plants in the surrounding inland lanes are different as well. The shoreward shingle is a garden of beautiful wild flowers, the most striking of them the yellow horned poppy. It is a plant whose dominating features are curves: in the diaphanous golden petals of the flowers, the bluish-green stems carrying silver-grey indented leaves, most of all in the long seedpod, which can be up to twelve inches when full-grown, tipped with a heart-shaped anther. The poppies are accompanied by quite a kitchen-garden of sea radish and sea carrot, and other flowers here include bird's foot trefoil, the little tough rest-harrow whose clinging tendrils enforced rest on old-fashioned harrow tines, the rough hawksbit, mouse-ear hawkweed, and sea campion.

On the landward side among low gorse and brambles bearing huge blackberry crops is hogweed, many grasses, the semi-parasitic little eyebright and parasitic broomrape and the dodder that covers the gorse, and sometimes viper's bugloss with wonderful gentian-blue flowers.

The Lower Ley shore harbours a profusion of plants, many of them aromatic, like the water mint, and the labiates: marsh woundwort, whose soft leaves were used to dress wounds, and the self-heal that was a cure-all. Many of these are purplish or pink; the bright blue of skullcap makes a good contrast. Above the smaller plants rise the great reed-beds that cover about a third of the Lower Ley and are being used again for thatching; there are different varieties as well: the common reed, bullrush, reedmace and spike rush live in harmony here. Across the marshy bottom of Ireland Bay on the north side of the Lower Ley there are a bridge and a wooden causeway through the rustling reeds, where a sudden swish or plop gives away the presence of a water bird. From the bridge can be seen beds of flags and that fine plant, the bog bean, rising from the water on its fleshy stems.

The Ley is one of the most frequented resorts for birds in Devon, ideal as a stopping place on spring and autumn migration, as shelter, larder with plentiful stocks of fish and other foodstuffs, and breeding ground; the adjacent sea, shore, woods and fields complete its avian amenities. The Field Centre makes valuable studies of birdlife as well as of plants and animals. 233 bird species have been recorded on the reserve, land and water birds, natives and on-passage migrants. They include gulls and terns of various kinds, gannets, grebes and herons, ducks, geese and swans, exotica such as the arctic skua, the melodious warbler and the blue-throat; many birds of prey, though mostly buzzards; and ravens live in Hartshorn Plantation. The duck are the most easily observable, they congregate at the south-west corner of the Ley near the road; and swan families rule on the opposite side of the lake, keeping order over birds and humans alike.

Local tradition still acknowledges an estuary near Strete Gate at the bottom of the hill below Strete village. The Gara valley here is level now and very marshy and the little river a mere stream that meanders with small bends and divisions through the lush grasses, gilded in spring with huge kingcups in clumps between giant mare's tails. One day Colin Gill drove us in the Land-Rover along the track on the east side of the valley to where a causeway crosses the marsh. The river runs on the west side here and there is an old bridge over it. In the woods nearby is a range of disused slate quarries, beautiful pinkish slate with a velvety sheen, but very brittle. The quarry sides are precipitous, going back into the steep hillside and overhung with gnarled ivied trees. There are some ruined quarrymen's cottages here, and a very solid wall above the river bank. What could this have been but the wall of a wharf for ships loading slate to moor at? It looks as if the estuary had been deep enough for this some centuries back, and the boats might have been taken through an outlet from the Higher Ley to the sea, or through both leys to the one at Torcross, which is now an underground culvert.

On that spring day we also drove through the lanes that lead off the ridgeway road from the Iron Age fort of Stanborough camp, a perfect oval earthwork crowned by windswept beeches with a vast view to Dartmoor north and the sea south, some miles south to Slapton and the wooded reaches of the Gara valley a couple of miles north of the quarries. It is a deeply remote place with a timeless air. We drove along grass rides perched on precipitous, thickly wooded hillsides. In places the bank was crumbling and the Land-Rover slithered and bumped about in pioneer fashion. Yet this wild and hidden place turned out to have been guested by two rising celebrities at the turn of this century: Jack Yeats the artist/writer, and John

Masefield the poet. Snail's Castle is on the east side of the valley, a romantic thatched cottage among the trees that was the home of Jack Yeats and his wife from 1897 to 1910, named by Yeats in Gaelic Cashlauna Shelmiddy. There is always a thriving population of snails in this lushly verdant and watery region.

Yeats, who was related to the Pollexfens of Brixham, started to draw and paint seriously in Devon, and a number of his racing scenes come from his visits to Totnes and other local race meetings; in those days every town and many villages had their own race course, as well as their pack of hounds.

In April 1903 his friend John Masefield came to stay at Snail's Castle. After his adventurous life on board sailing ships and in America, Masefield had established himself as a writer in London, and at the time he visited Jack Yeats was engaged to be married. His letters to his fiancée record the carefree days he spent in Devon, teaching Yeats sailors' jargon, going for long walks and watching sailing ships off Slapton Sands and at Kingsbridge and Salcombe.

Much of their time was spent in boys' pursuits, making and sailing model ships on the Gara below Snail's Castle. They both wrote about this. In 1910 Yeats published a small book, *A Little Fleet*, that describes five ships, a fore and aft schooner, a paddle steamboat, a fireship, a topsail schooner, and a brig, made from bits of wood or cardboard boxes. Yeats illustrated them and made a chart of the Gara, including landmarks like Buccaneers Gallows, Desolate Deadmen's Teeth, Bad Snags and so on. He wrote: "The owners and myself are indebted to the Fleet Poet for the verses throughout the book." Masefield did not over-exert himself to provide such rhymes as:

> And now by Gara rushes,
>   When stars are blinking white;
> And sleep has stilled the thrushes,
>   And sunset brings the night;
>
> There, where the stones are gleamin',
>   A passer-by can hark
> To the old drowned "Monte" seamen
>   A-singing through the dark. . . .

But he stored away the old tales and traditions about the district, including the Gara valley, to make use of in later books. In 1911 he published the children's novel *Jim Davis*. It is a racy, well-told smuggling tale set in the district and full of local detail. The two boys in the story are portraits of Yeats and Masefield in their games of sailing model boats on the Gara, and Snail's Castle is the hero's uncle's house, a mile from the sea above a trout-stream that "rose about three miles from my uncle's house, in a boggy wood full of springs. Below my uncle's house it was full of little falls, with great mossy boulders which checked its flow, and pools where the bubbles spun. . . ." In this stretch the Gara is much wider than in the delta valley. Masefield describes the valley and the old quarries, and the great sea-caves at Blackpool Sands are his smugglers' hiding-place. The place made a deep impression upon him and several of his poems were inspired by the South Hams, including *The Tarry Buccaneer* and *Christmas 1903*, that mentions Salcombe.

The Gara actually rises about eight miles inland, south of Halwell. Its course, a miniature version of the larger rivers, takes it through some of the richest and remotest farmlands of the South Hams, and under little old stone bridges whose narrow span keeps big lorries away from the deep lanes; they have evocative names like Battle Bridge and Deer Bridge. The Gara is still the trout stream that Masefield loved. I met a small boy fishing at Deer Bridge, with a moderate-sized trout proudly displayed beside him. Life here runs in accord with the seasons, at the pace it should.

Half a mile inland from the Ley is Slapton village sheltering at the foot of a steep hill, compact and threaded with narrow old streets between the thatched cottages with their bright miniature gardens. As in other villages in the area, some of their fat chimney stacks lean drowsily, all in the same direction. I am told that this is due to subsidence in the mortar, presumably aided by the prevailing winds. It does not prevent the chimneys from functioning and matches the rounded outer walls of some of the cottages. The church spire is companioned by the neighbouring tall thirteenth-century tower that is all that remains of Sir Guy de Brien's collegiate chantry, its solid square crumbling now at the grass-grown summit, its hexagonal side tower capped by an attractive small pinnacle. Below its owl-haunted height stands the ancient Tower Inn.

At the west end of Slapton Sands is Torcross village, the first of two old coastal settlements that could almost be termed beach settlements, set perilously close to the inundating sea, whose plentiful fish drew people away from the safety of the harbours to live along its unprotected shore. At Tinsey Head over a mile beyond Torcross to the west is the dividing line between Dartmouth slates and the schist layer stretching westward to Bolt Tail that gives the magnificent cliff profiles which make sailing into Salcombe harbour so memorable whatever the weather.

A mile west of Tinsey Head is the second shore settlement, the totally ruined village of Hallsands. For centuries it had been a fishing village with a population of over a hundred living in cottages built on a marine platform just above the same shingle bank that forms Slapton Sands. Its ruin was brought about through thoughtless interference with the delicate natural balance controlling the shingle bank. In 1897 dredging of the underwater shingle off Hallsands was begun for use in building an extension to the naval dockyard at Devonport. Despite protests and predictions of disaster by the Hallsands residents, over 650,000 tons of gravel were dredged from the seabed. The beach level began to subside soon after the dredging stopped, and in 1903 houses began to be undermined and part of the one road through the village collapsed. Repairs were made and not much more happened until 1917, when violent storms in January completely destroyed twenty-nine houses. The villagers escaped with their lives and most of their possessions and were eventually rehoused on higher ground a little inland, all except for one tenacious lady, Elizabeth Prettejohn, who lived on in the one remaining habitable house until her death in 1964. Now only a few dangerously undermined scraps of wall and some foundations are left of Hallsands.

As Start Point is rounded an astoundingly changed cliff landscape meets the gaze: the majestic jagged schist heights rise ever higher to Prawle Point over five miles away across Lannacombe Bay. A rock, The Island, detached from the mainland, marks this southernmost point of Devon. The gap between it and the cliff has trapped many ships that have miscalculated their bearings on the upchannel voyage, even recently, despite the presence of the white-painted coastguard station on the windswept headland. Just beyond Prawle Point there is a small bay with golden sand divided by a

promontory into two halves. The cliffs loom hugely above its deep
waters, bounded on the west by the sheer rise of Gammon Head.
Further along are porcine Ham Stone and Pig's Nose. The bay is a
beautiful anchorage for swimming, possessing a completely different atmosphere from other beaches nearer roads, supremely fresh
and self-sufficient, tolerating human visitation only in the deceptive
calm of summer. This is the season when the path along these cliffs,
part of the almost continuous South Devon coastal path, seems like
a walk through a divinely planted rock garden, patterned in a
perfect blend of order and casualness. There are beds of bluebells
high up below the gorse, followed by foxgloves, then the flowers
grow graded in size so that lower down are cushions of pink thrift
and the neat little blue heads of the spring squill. In summer smaller
flowers predominate: buoyant patches of wild thyme flanked by
wild mint, sky-blue small scabious and sheep's bit, and everywhere
the stonecrop with its ruddy, fleshy little leaves and minute starry
white flowers, our equivalent to the cacti of desert places. In many
places on the cliffs near sea level, doggedly rooting in rock crevices,
grows the samphire whose culling Shakespeare describes in *King
Lear*: 'Halfway down hangs one that gathers samphire, dreadful
trade." Its grey-green leaves put out fleshy points from the tough
stem, the flowers are yellow florets rising from a collared stem, each
floret with its own green collar. The pungent leaves can be blanched
and added discreetly to salads.

August used to find the cliffs purpled with heather; now, one
hopes at least only temporarily, bracken has strangled it and the
slopes are green all summer, until the bracken turns its warm
chestnut in October. This flower garden is a delectable home for
various butterfly species; some typical examples are small coppers,
silver-studded blues and pearl-bordered fritillaries. Among the
rock crevices lizards and slow-worms make their homes, and
occasionally an adder may be seen sunbathing. Subfusc beetles
trundle across the path, and ubiquitous stonechats flit among the
gorse bushes, watched from above by a kestrel or hen harrier. On
rocks near the sea groups of shags or cormorants stand in rows
resting after fishing, one or two with wings heraldically outstretched to dry. Gulls nest on crazy ledges, there are numbers of
Greater Black-Backs here, huge, fierce and handsome, with the
coldest of gold eyes and formidable scimitar bills.

Most boats make for the Bar across the harbour entrance at Salcombe, flanked on the west by the highest point, Bolt Head, beyond Starehole Bay. The cliffs maintain their formidable loftiness for another five miles to Bolt Tail, where Bigbury Bay begins.

Along just one mile of this coast 140 wrecks have been charted. One of the most famous was that of HMS *Ramillies* on the night of 15 February 1760. She was a ship of the line carrying ninety guns out of Plymouth. With other ships she had been blown off course in a gale and confused Bolt Tail with Rame Head; she saw the danger too late and after a brave struggle was driven on to the rocks and sunk. Only twenty-six of her crew of 734 escaped with their lives; a few objects from the ship have been salvaged, but it is reputed that one of her cannon lies in a cave nearby. One very calm day we were able to row in there from the sloop. We didn't find the cannon but the cave was a wonder of green and red shining rocks, lit by a slit high up in the cave-roof. It is a special privilege to be allowed access to the sea's secret places, and one I always prize.

On stormy nights we recall the *Ramillies* in the old ballad, "The Loss of the *Ramillies*".

> It was on one day, one certain day,
> When the Ramillies at her anchor lay,
> That very night a gale came on,
> And our ship from her anchorage away did run.
>
> The rain poured down in terrible drops,
> The sea broke over our fore-top,
> With our yards and canvas neatly spread,
> We were thinking to weather the old Ram's Head.
>
> Our bosun cried "My hearties all,
> Listen unto me while I blow my call,
> Launch out your boats your lives to save
> Or the seas this night will be your grave."
>
> Then overboard our boats we tossed,
> So many got in that most was lost;
> There was some in one place, some in another,
> The watch down below – they all was smothered.

Sad news, sad news to Plymouth came
That the Ramillies was lost and all her men,
Excepting two that told the tale;
How that ship behaved in that dreadful gale.

Come all you pretty maids and weep with me
For the loss of your true loves in the Ramillies;
All Plymouth town it flowed with tears,
When they heard the news of that sad affair.

Another dramatic wreck on this coast was the *Herzogin Cecilie*, a Finnish tea-clipper on one of the last voyages from Australia with grain. In a fog on 25 April 1936 she hit the Ham Stone off Soar Mill Cove a couple of miles west of Bolt Head, and then grounded at Water Cove. It was found possible after some of the cargo had been unloaded to tow her into Starehole Bay, Bolt Head. But salvage operations stopped there, and the ship turned into a tourist attraction, with boat trips organized by her skipper from Salcombe. The rest of the cargo spilled out and contaminated all the Salcombe beaches that year with stinking, rotting grain. In the winter storms the back of this romantic full-rigged ship was gradually broken, and over many years she disintegrated and was dismantled. Her timbers were used to make ornaments, her rigging rotted, her ironwork rusted. A small piece of her still lies on the sand underwater in Starehole Bay, a practice diving ground for beginners from the diving school.

Tucked in behind Bolt Tail is Hope Cove, the small village that used to stand for lobsters and cob cottages. There is little lobster fishing here now, but the cottages stand plump, crisply white and opulent under their curved bouffant thatched heads. They are perfect examples of the art of cob-building, after stone the most typical material for vernacular architecture in Devon. Cob houses are sophisticated mud-huts, for cob is a mixture of clay soil, pebbles, straw and water, sometimes bound into a caking mixture with cow dung and hair. It was kneaded by being trodden by animal or human feet, with water added from the nearest source until the mix was fairly soft. The walls were built up on a stone plinth, in two-foot layers that were each left to dry before the next was added. They could be up to four feet thick, and when carefully built they are watertight and well-insulated, a thousand times better than the low-cost drab building developments of today that often resemble wheelless caravans.

A mile west of Hope is Thurlestone Rock, an outlier from the shallow ledges of slate pushing off the shore east of Thurlestone Sands, that provide the endless interest of rock pools. Thurlestone means the "pierced stone" and its natural archway is a familiar landmark. Its motto "Bear every shock like Thurlestone Rock" still holds good after some of the worst gales on record. Like Hope and Bantham, Thurlestone village has fine cob cottages, contrasted with Thurlestone Hotel above the golf course like a stranded liner from the 1930s, and a handsome church. Strange folk legends linger here. Mark Bawden, the curate of Malborough who replied to Dean Jeremiah Milles's questionnaire to parishes in the 1750s, also transcribed Mr Reed's notes on Thurlestone, "at his request, as his was much blotted", and Mr Reed, the Vicar, gave some odd information in his reply. He says that some fields, called the Sentries, had been held by the Danes or Saxons, where watch was kept. "On Midsummer Day tis currently said that the Danes having before killed the husbands in order to gain their wives to themselves, these brave women had a secret watchword concerning roosticocks so well communicated to each other, that the same night every bloody ravisher was sacrificed in revenge of the double injurious treatment upon which tis said that at the annual return of that eve great fires were made in several parts of the parish with great rejoicing, a custom in some degree retained to this time. The Eve of the Epiphany too according to tradition was famous for an entire expulsion of the Danes by a decisive battle on the Ham [Bantham]: a large spot of common ground by the seaside where the dead were buried, and some now living say that their parents or other old people affirmed that multitudes of human bones have been seen there which on some accidental occasion had been thrown up and shewn as undoubted evidence of that matter of fact or somewhat like it, and indeed comparing that part of the Ham with the rest of it a stranger might by some circumstantials credit such a story without the imputation of being too credulous. I shall mention one thing more because so singular that I cannot learn this used anywhere else, most of the children the day following Innocents either go or if too little are borne round the parish to every house capable of giving, and a set of words being gabbled by one and all with a confused noise each without exception receives a Boon of one sort or another and then is sent to another place to partake of a further Bounty. This custom is immemorial some imagining that it has not only reference to Innocents Day but a particular deliverance from an intended massacre here."

On flat beaches like Thurlestone Sands the wreckers would carry out their grim work, luring ships on to the rocks. One horrid tale is of a lady on board the ship *Chantiloupe*, thus wrecked in 1722. She dressed in all her silks and jewels hoping to be rescued, only to be murdered by the wreckers and her mutilated body buried in the sand. It was later dug up by a dog and the murderers given chase but not apprehended, although the victim was given Christian burial. The dark tales and lost traditions add to the region's air of mystery that fascinates me by its very contrast with the sunny benignity of the South Hams summer and the matter-of-fact humour and goodwill of most Devonians.

Another contrast meets us a mile further west in the sizeable breakers of Bantham Sands, the only possible surfing place along this coast. At the east side of the beach there are dangerous currents, but the main part affords good sport at the right tide times. The mouth of the Avon ends Bantham beach with a sand spit, and immediately east of it is Burgh Island. As at St Michael's Mount a chapel was dedicated to St Michael on top of this steep outcrop. It was replaced by a pleasure house long disappeared, and then became a huer's hut for the lookout who raised the hue and cry when a shoal of pilchards was sighted. You can walk across the sand to the island at low tide; when it is high a sea tractor runs a ferry service in summer. From the summit of the island one can look back across the bay to Bolt Tail, and westward over to Rame Head beyond Plymouth, a clear view of sea and skyscape pointed only by gulls or a gannet and purposeful distant white sails.

A mile up the road northward from Bigbury Beach on the west bank of the Avon mouth the village of Bigbury is presided over by its good church and the ancient walls of the farmyard of Bigbury Court, the old manor, whose former status is shown by the fine circular dovecot in the middle of the large courtyard, disused but with some of its wooden furnishings still *in situ*. Here lives Bill

Bowden-Smith, a historian whose father was rector here early this century, and who built a house on a site with a breathtaking view. It is just below the top of the ridge on the west bank of the Avon mouth. You can see the whole S-bend of the river mouth, the village of Bantham, the Ham with its sand dunes, the Sands and the further ridge before Thurlestone.

Half a mile further west along the road from Bigbury Court brings you to a crossroads and the hamlet of St Ann's Chapel. What is slightly confusingly called "The Pickwick Inn" is in fact part of a fourteenth-century chapel. Vincent Piper, the landlord, told me one of those stories that are agony to hear: when a blocked-up wall space was opened during alterations to the house in the 1930s, a chest containing old books and documents was found. The then owners felt that no one could want that sort of old rubbish and threw it on the bonfire. It is the kind of loss that is grievous, details of the history of a unique place gone up in smoke like Hardy's letters; but, in a somewhat similar way to Hardy's novels, the house remains to tell a different story to everyone who comes to see it or live in it. The Pipers have a remarkable home, with their bedroom in the chapel itself, an upper room made at some date out of the one-storey little church, with medieval cruck roof timbers. This room is reputed to have been used as a meeting place for the Royalists of the area, who gathered here from neighbouring manor houses.

Vincent Piper believes that the holy well of St Ann's, that is generally held to be where the underground stream emerges in a field east of the inn and road, was once in the inn cellar, where the stream still runs, although blocked off. St Ann was a Celtic goddess famed for her partiality for babies as a delicacy in her diet (the decapitated heads were thrown into her wells, as evidence in the form of skulls has disclosed). The Church legitimized pagan saints by building churches on their religious sites, including so-called holy wells. This may be what happened here.

The lane south of St Ann's leads to another ancient village, Ringmore. Here is a fine church, romantic cob cottages with flowery gardens, and two old farmsteads. The "Journey's End" is an ancient smugglers' inn where R. C. Sherriff wrote his play of that name. The smugglers had to walk up from the sea a mile away at Ayrmer Cove. The Dartmouth slate cliffs here are among the most beautiful in our region. The schist of Bolt Head and Tail are wild and grand, the Meadfoot Beds that follow them made the beaches and lower lands of Thurlestone and Bantham, now the Dartmouth slates run from Ayrmer Cove to Andern Point in the Sound. The slate is so striking in this area because it lies in huge smooth slabs on the cliff-face, sometimes for almost the whole height in one unbroken face. When the morning sun shines on the slate it can be a dazzling mirror; when the sun moves round, the slate gleams with a lustrous sheen in pink or greenish shades. The marine platform below the cliffs has been ridged and furrowed into strange swirls and convolutions by water action, and its colours are in waves of pinks, silvers and greens. Another fascinating feature here is the presence of fossils, from here to the other side of the Erme estuary. Although the geologists complain of their poor state of preservation they are good enough for an amateur, and I was pleased when I found an impression of the spine of a pteraspid ostracoderm in a beautiful heart-shaped piece of pink slate the size and thickness of the palm of my hand. This six-inch-long fish lived over four hundred million years ago in the Devonian or Silurian period.

It is an easy climb along the marine platform to the Cathedral Cave at Hoist Point, a favourite place of Bill Bowden-Smith, where he proposed to his future wife. You can go in one side of it and out of the other, passing from light to dark and again to light. The cave is high enough to walk upright in, and the clear water of the open sea is especially inviting to swimmers here after the scramble along the rocks. Few other people come to disturb the rich solitude. The only thing that must be timed carefully on this excursion is the state of the tide; if not in a boat you must start out half an hour before low water so as not to risk getting cut off, as the cliffs are almost unscalable here.

Beacon Point, about a mile west of Ayrmer Cove, is, surprisingly, sandstone. A narrow mile-long intrusion, Scobbiscombe Sandstones, divides two slate variations, Wembury Siltstones to east, and Yealm formation to west, and runs north-east from Beacon Point, past Scobbiscombe Farm to Kingston village. Its effect seen on the point is like an alien giant whose skin is loose scree instead of smooth and layered slate, and the cliff path here feels perilous and exposed. But once passed and in slate country, again the beautiful mouth of the Erme and Mothecombe Beach welcome with their grey-pink sides and golden sands, and the cliffs continue, their contour changed by several steep green hung valleys before the first coastal section of the Nine Mile Drive and Stoke Point. Around it Stoke Bay is a small cove at the end of an almost dry valley, with a small family caravan site that fills the sheltered little bay and is divided into two parts by an alder coppice. At the lower edge of the coppice, right on the low cliff edge, is the Church of St Peter the Poor Fisherman. A charter of 1225 gives the first written mention of it, but what stands now is fourteenth-century with a fifteenth-century aisle and porch. It is not a landmark like St Werburgh's at Wembury and hardly noticeable as you sail past. But walking the coastal path it is a delight to come upon; it has an air of benevolent sanctity and contentment with its incongruous site among the caravans. Recently two of its missing roofs were renewed with timbers and slates, the walls stripped of ivy and repaired. The central area of the church is still roofless, but this seems merely to add to its grace: a place of prayer in God's fresh air. In an ancient niche somebody young keeps flowers and tokens of faith and care; on the floor underneath this is a plaque commemorating Kate Greenwood, 1909–75, "who loved and saved this church". The door is always open and services are held sometimes in summer. Yet at nearby St Werburgh the door is kept locked against the visitor as well as the vandal, and I had to visit Holbeton three times before gaining access to the church.

The coastal path continues westward from Stoke following the Nine Mile Drive along the Warren, one of a number where rabbits were bred as they were on Dartmoor, and where Stoke Warren Cottage witnesses to the one-time home of the keeper. The walk rounds Gara Point and drops down through rhododendron and oak woods beside the mouth of the Yealm, the last river before Plymouth Sound. On the other side of Yealm mouth Great Mewstone lies ahead off Wembury Point. Like Warren, Mewstone is a ubiquitous place-name along the gull-haunted South Devon coast: there are Great and Little Mew Stones off Bolt Head and Mew Stone off the east side of Dartmouth, most of them nesting-places for the seabirds. Fulmars and kittiwakes breed on the Wembury Mewstone. The rock is shaped like a right-angled triangle with the sea-line the hypotenuse. It looks austere and is uninhabited, although people have lived on it in the past. I remember it on a windless day when the sea-fog suddenly enveloped us and we were becalmed and blinded. When a subaqueous booming indicated a submarine passing beneath us my husband got into the dinghy and towed the yacht along with the aid of the compass. We began to hear hidden voices from a crowd of people, eerily invisible. Suddenly the mist lifted and showed us the Mewstone only a few yards away, and Wembury Beach covered with holiday-makers in bright sunshine. We scuttled into Newton Ferrers harbour before the mist came down again.

Wembury is only five miles from Plymouth, but still in many respects remains a secluded village in an impressive setting. The church tower has been a landmark for approaching sailors for many centuries. St Werburgh, "the holy daughter of that pagan Wolphor, King of Mercia, standeth close upon the sea clifts", half a mile west of Yealm mouth and almost due north of the Eddystone Lighthouse fourteen miles out in the Channel. We were at Wembury on an April Easter Monday afternoon when it was warm enough, out of the chill north-easterly, to bask on the grassy slope below the churchyard with a clear view of the lighthouse. Early yachts were making for Newton Ferrers over one of those absurdly calm seas of spring, gulls wheeled, shags skimmed the surface, wet-suited children splashed off Wembury beach below, all was peace except that on Wembury Point below HMS *Cambridge* a slim, menacing gun pointed seaward. Behind us stood the square church tower, the slightly higher stair turret pointing up its symmetry, its cap feathered with a pair of jackdaws who stayed there all the time hardly moving. The low church doors on the south and east have rough granite arches, and the church has good monuments to the Heles and Calmadys. The cliffside churchyard is densely populated except for a few corners already booked for future occupants! There are gravestones from the seventeenth century onwards, many of purple slate. One Calmady daughter was "dearly loved and deeply mourned", she died in a particularly hard Victorian winter having "devoted her life to the poor", and one can imagine her struggling through snowdrifts carrying soups and jellies to suffering villagers. In fact, from the seventeenth century this area had a particularly large number of paupers.

It was in 1683 that Sir Warwick Hele built the Hele Almshouses

in Wembury village. They are a perfectly proportioned complex
with an unspoilt original frontage. There are four houses in the
row and incorporated in their centre is the chapel, with barrel-
vaulted ceiling and large windows. Nan Kelly, one of the present
residents, showed me round and invited me into her own house.
She knows people who remember when church services for
Wembury were held in the almshouse chapel and people queued
up along the lane to pack into the little building, the men in
bowlers, with spats and sticks. What stories the residents then
could have told, and all of them through the centuries, their
versions of the lives of the Heles at Wembury House and Thorn
and the Calmadys at Langdon Court more colourful than official
family histories.

The elements, the powers of nature, are sensed more strongly in
Devonshire; the summer calms are more intensely idyllic, the sea
clearer, its surface a flat window looking down on to the mysterious
mirror-world of plants, creatures and caves, but with the menace of
change ever present, the memory of unpredictable temper always
there. The element of surprise is endemic: a sudden black triangle
ahead of the boat that announces a basking shark, the uncanny
stirring and frilling of an otherwise calm sea that denotes a mackerel
shoal, freakish squalls, rainbows and astounding sunsets. The
reassurances are clearer: the succession of lighthouse signals and
leading lights, the heat of becalmed August, the boisterous breezes
that make sailing exhilaration and to look up at the mast holding the
striving sail perfection.

All odours are stronger here: rain smells fresher, snow can be
sniffed in the presaging east wind of January, mist as well as sun
enhances flower scents, bog, mud, and farmyard smells are more
pungent, our winter fires are fuelled with winey resinous cupressus
logs whose wood is so white and fine-grained it seems cruel to burn
it.

To spend time on the sea passing the varying beauty of the coast,
or on land among curving hills, deep valleys, powerful moors and
towns at ease with themselves is a privilege I prize.

Chapter Nine

PLYMOUTH – PORT OF ENTERPRISES

THE PROPER WAY to approach the largest city in Devon is from the sea, where every fathom and nautical mile is a full tide of history. Plymouth Sound is by far the biggest harbour entrance in the South-west, and the estuaries of the St Germans, Tamar and Tavy rivers are wide and, with the Sound and the smaller estuary of the Plym on the east, provide unlimited fine anchorages for ships of all sizes, from warships to windsurfers. The Sound itself was exposed to south-westerly winds until the breakwater was built to shelter it in the early nineteenth century; during the medieval period Dartmouth was the safer anchorage. But the influential presence in Plymouth of men like Sir Francis Drake, who made it his home port, his kinsman Sir John Hawkins, treasurer to and comptroller of the Navy in the sixteenth century, John Davis the navigator from Dartmouth, the three Gilberts and their half-brother, Sir Walter Raleigh, and Sir Richard Grenville, assured Plymouth's expansion from then on. As William Browne of Tavistock wrote in *Britannia's Pastorals*:

> Time never can produce men to o'ertake
> The fames of Grenville, Davis, Gilbert, Drake
> Or worthy Hawkins . . .

Today the huge county borough of Plymouth spreads across and far up the peninsula formed by the Plym and the Tavy, and Plymstock and Plympton on the east bank of the Plym are now part of the city. The site has been in use since the Bronze Age, when an even earlier ridgeway ran from Sutton Pool to Dartmoor; a trading settlement existed at Mount Batten, the point opposite the Barbican, from 1000 BC till the end of the Roman period. There were Celtic, Saxon and Norman settlers.

During the Middle Ages the Saxon priory at Plympton had control over the little town, until gradually the merchants took over. Plymouth grew out of the merging of three small towns, Plymouth on the east, Devonport, originally called Dock, on the west, and Stonehouse in between; these are still fairly distinct areas. It has probably experienced more naval military history than any other English city except London. The defeat of the Spanish Armada is still everywhere in mind, there was considerable fighting over Plymouth during the Civil War, innumerable naval fleets have set sail from and returned to Plymouth, including part of the Falkland Islands Task Force in 1982. Charles II's star-shaped citadel still stands in essence as the seventeenth-century fortress that replaced earlier fortifications.

In the Sound about 400 yards offshore lies Drake's Island, a six-acre knoll of volcanic ash and tuff with a small limestone area on its south-facing side. A passenger ferry runs from the West Pier at Sutton Pool, calling at the island and then going on to the landing stage for Mount Edgcumbe, since Tudor times the home of the Edgcumbe family and now a country park. In summer as you step ashore on the island the chief impression is of freshness and fragrance. The path leads past the adventure centre that a decade ago took over the old military buildings built, at various periods, of silver-grey limestone, and the labyrinth of defensive tunnels and passages that warren the crown of the island. There is a fine chronological record of land/sea defences for military historians to observe here. Originally named St Nicholas's Island from a chapel on its summit demolished in the sixteenth century, it was given Drake's name when he became governor of the island in about 1583. It was garrisoned continuously until recently.

Yet its character has withstood all the manoeuvres and delving and gunnery and now the ecology of the island is zealously conserved. Scots pines lend the air an added tang, fennel and mint grow wild amidst sea campion, thrift and yarrow, and many varieties of grasses ripple in the sea breeze.

The island summit is a magnificent viewpoint. To the south beyond the breakwater is the Channel; to the east Staddon Heights and just south-west of them Bovisand Bay, where there is another magnificent fortress constructed for defence against the Napoleonic threat, and now a deep-sea diving school. There is a twin stout defence-work on the opposite, west shore at Picklecombe Point; this is being converted into holiday apartments!

From here you can watch the constant variation of shipping moving about the Sound: warships, the Roscoff and St Malo ferries, pleasure craft and local ferries, and all manner of yachts, small sailing boats, canoes, kayaks and windsurfers. And despite the bristling fortifications of centuries, the modern naval base and city architecture, the grandeur and beauty of the city's natural setting survive.

The panorama of Plymouth from the island is incomparable. Some of the Dockyard buildings can be seen beyond Devil's Point on the west. East of them the streets of Stonehouse rise above modern Stonehouse Dock where the continental ferries berth. The sun still catches the slate and limestone of the houses and makes them shine as it did when Celia Fiennes first saw Plymouth at the end of the seventeenth century: "The houses all built of this marble and the slate at the top looks like lead and glisters in the sun."

Then in the centre is the emerald sweep of the Hoe's limestone rise, backed by the fine façades of the elegant houses in Citadel Road. Immediately right of the Hoe rise the massive walls of the Citadel and beyond them is the inlet of Sutton Pool, Plymouth's first harbour, where the trawler fleet moors near the Fish Market, the other side of the West Pier and Mayflower Steps.

Whether from the island or the Hoe, landlubbers have been watching the movement of ships in and out of this generous anchorage for close on a thousand years. The Hawkinses, John and his merchant father William, Humphrey, John and Adrian Gilbert, Martin Frobisher, Richard Grenville, all set sail from Plymouth on voyages of discovery or war. Towering over them in renown are the two greatest Devonians of all, Sir Francis Drake (1542–1595) and Sir Walter Raleigh (1552–1618) and thus ten years Drake's junior. Their lives make a fascinating comparison.

Both men were born on farms, to fathers who were tenants of good standing. Drake's parents were stout Protestants, and when the Marian Catholic disturbances brought danger to their district, Tavistock, they moved to Kent, where Francis and his eleven brothers were brought up, for some of the time on a hulk on the Medway. Raleigh was born at Hayes Barton in east Devon, where he was brought up. His family was higher in the social scale than Drake's, although they were distantly related, like most of the leading Devonshire families. Walter's mother was Katherine

Champernowne, sister of Sir Arthur Champernowne, a Vice-Admiral; she was Walter's father's third wife, and the widow of Otho Gilbert of Compton, with whom she had three sons, Walter's half-brothers John, Humphrey and Adrian.

While Drake returned to his home county, Raleigh never settled in Devon in adult life. It was typical of the age for boys to leave the safety of home early. Drake went to sea in his teens, and Raleigh at fourteen went to France to fight with a cousin who had married a Frenchwoman, for the Huguenots against the Catholics. The pattern of their lives was set as early as this: Drake's life was chiefly spent in voyaging; Raleigh, although deeply concerned with maritime affairs, spent relatively little time at sea, not for lack of inclination or courage, but often because he was kept at court by the Queen. Great man though he was, two of his four voyages, whose purpose was to search for gold in Guiana, were unsuccessful in their chief aim, although they provided knowledge of other lands and peoples that Raleigh wrote about brilliantly.

Drake was the epitome of the Elizabethan seaman: he was the defender of his country, explorer and discoverer, adventurer, buccaneer, corsair, a man of action and war who was also, as mariners then had to be, a fine artist who drew his own charts as he covered new seas and routes. Above all he was a superb sailor and an immortal credit to his maritime county. His feats of seamanship have never been equalled, with his great circumnavigation of the world in 1577–80, his many forays in the frail, awkward yet re-markably agile little ships against the great Spanish and Portuguese craft, and his leading part in the defeat of the Armada in 1588 after the famous singeing of the King of Spain's beard at Cadiz in 1587.

Raleigh was a soldier, courtier, politician, for many years the chief protector of his Queen, romantic lover, father and poet. Both men had the Elizabethan's strong ambition for fame and wealth. Drake literally took most of his wealth by privateering, Raleigh's came largely through gifts from the Queen, that were lost when the tide of favour turned against him. Although Drake chanced his luck a few times by harrying Spanish ships when Elizabeth was contemplating a settlement with Spain, his career was relatively free from the setbacks suffered by Raleigh, which were largely caused by his own imprudent actions. In the end, most of Raleigh's fame derives from his charismatic personality – typically expressed in his deep love for the Queen – a love that was as passionate as courtesy, convention and Elizabeth herself would allow, and which occasioned many of his finest poems (there is no doubt of the veracity of the famous cloak episode); also from his patriotic love of country in the context of Elizabethan politics and statecraft; and his love of the land. Like Drake's, Raleigh's father had not owned his land, and Raleigh achieved his aim of doing so, both in great Irish estates and then the Castle, with extensive manors, of Sherborne, given him by the Queen; and from his love of the many branches of learning opening out in his lifetime and practised by himself and his intellectual friends at Durham House on the Thames in London, another residence provided for him by Elizabeth.

But Raleigh tempted fate, in the person of kings, too far. He married his great love, Bess Throckmorton, secretly, in defiance of the Queen's sure disapproval, and consequently he and Bess spent five years in the Tower. Then, on the death of his beloved Queen, James I clapped him back there and only released him to sail on the doomed second voyage to Guiana. The outcome – failure to find the gold of El Dorado – was foreseeable, but Raleigh once more demonstrated his romantically gallant nature in returning to England, instead of settling elsewhere in safety, to face certain execution. It is impossible not to admire him, and we may be grateful in a sense for the long years of imprisonment when he wrote many of his poems and his *History of the World*.

When Drake knew himself to be dying of "the bludy flix" (dysentery) on the *Golden Hind* off Puerto Rico on *his* ill-fated last voyage, that also saw the death of Sir John Hawkins who sailed with him, he had himself dressed in his armour to sign his last will. His last words have not come down to us; Raleigh dramatized the prelude to his execution as beautifully as could have been expected. He asked to test the sharpness of the axe and said: "This is a sharp medicine, but it is a sure cure for all diseases," and urged on the executioner's faltering hands. In command of himself to the end, the previous evening Raleigh had written out in the flyleaf of his Bible an old poem to which he added two new lines:

> Even such is Time which takes in trust
> Our youth, our joys and all we have,
> And pays us but with age and dust,

Who in the dark and silent grave
When we have wandered all our ways
Shuts up the story of our days.
And from which earth and grave and dust
The Lord shall raise me up I trust.

In comparison, the characters of these two great men emerge more clearly, so far as is possible with such complex personalities. Despite my sympathies for Raleigh as a poet I find myself putting Drake before him in my gallery of heroes and heroines. Raleigh is a hero for all England, his active years were spent mainly in London and his best-loved home was Sherborne. True, he was Lord Warden of the Stannaries and probably sat in judgement at the Stannary Parliament on Crockern Tor, and he was MP for Bosinney in Cornwall. He knew Plymouth well and took much care in preparing the land and sea defences against the Armada; he also donated his own vessel, the *Ark Royal*, to be Lord Howard, the Lord High Admiral's, flagship for the battle against the Armada.

But Drake was always a Devonian. As his fortunes rose he bought property in Looe Street, Plymouth, and later purchased Sir Richard Grenville's home, converted from a former Cistercian monastery, Buckland Abbey, near Yelverton, seven miles from Plymouth. Both his wives were Devonshire ladies. Drake became mayor of Plymouth and brought it a new water supply by having a leat cut to run from Dartmoor to the city. It was to Plymouth that he returned in triumph again and again. It is no wonder that his spirit lives on in his native city and that although he died childless and seems to have had little time for love, Plymothians today still walk the streets in his likeness with ruddy hair, cheeks and beards and piercing blue mariners' eyes.

Only two years after Raleigh's execution, in 1620, another famous departure took place at Plymouth when, to escape James I's hostility, the Pilgrim Fathers sailed from West Pier to settle in the New World that Drake and Raleigh had worked so hard to colonize for England. It was by chance that Plymouth was their last sight of England, for they had set sail from Southampton in two ships, the *Speedwell* and the *Mayflower*, but had been obliged to put in, first to Dartmouth, and then again to Plymouth, when

Speedwell sprang a persistent leak; she was disposed of and the little company crammed into the *Mayflower*.

The reconstructed voyages of this century in the exactly re-produced replicas of the *Golden Hinde* and the *Mayflower* have helped us to appreciate still more the dauntless spirit of the early mariners.

Plymouth continued to develop as a naval town after the end of the Elizabethan age. The hub of its prosperity until recent times was the Dockyard. It offered a large number of the citizens of Plymouth various types of shore employment connected with the building and maintenance of the ships of the Royal Navy. It is still an employer, but on a reduced scale now no ships are built here. At the end of the seventeenth century William III founded this new naval base, called merely Dock, to combat hostility from France. Not until 1824 was the name Devonport granted, and the area con-taining the dockyard itself and the surrounding streets was recognized as a separate town which was incorporated in 1837. It is situated west of Stonehouse, that also formed part of the early naval base with its grand buildings, the Royal Naval Hospital of 1761, the Royal Marine Barracks, 1784 onwards, and the Royal Victualling Yard, 1826–35.

The massive stone walls of the whole area withstood the air-raids of the 1940s to remain a monument to British sea-power. The oldest parts of the Dockyard are a fascinating museum of shipbuild-ing architecture, with several of the original, and first, stone docks and high yards still in existence along the banks of the Hamoaze, as this part of the Sound at the mouth of the Tamar/Tavy estuary is called. Perhaps the most impressive building is the remaining late eighteenth-century Ropery, originally 1200 feet long, although damaged in World War Two. The solidity of the limestone and iron used in this building is as great a marvel as the ropes and tackle that went into the construction of those great oaken ships whose pictures are displayed proudly on the walls of so many modern Plymouth buildings, that launch the imagination through un-charted regions.

Still in place and working order here is a gruesome reminder of the wars with the French: an interior gallows with stout noose and drop-floor. In complete contrast to this is a charming summer-house commemorating the visit of George III to the naval base, with slim white-painted columns and a concave roof, set on a grassy knoll and beautifully kept. The King climbed the knoll to get a view over the whole yard.

The Dockyard has expanded west along the Hamoaze with new docks that now service nuclear submarines, and the new enormous roofed-in frigate complex incorporating three older docks. Although most of the older docks are now silent and disused, the area is still the naval heart of Plymouth. Here where a total of 308 warships were built between 1694 and 1971, the great seafaring tradition is still much in evidence, whether it is celebrating the departure or arrival of intrepid single-handed sailors or the triumphant return of warships.

I cannot remember Plymouth before World War Two, but I do remember walking to the top of Bolt Head near Salcombe and watching the fires of its bombing lighting up the whole of the western sky. The naval base and city suffered the full fury of the Luftwaffe, over a thousand people died, nearly four thousand houses were destroyed and eighteen thousand seriously damaged; all the major civic buildings, some of them handsome nineteenth-century architecture, were gutted, and half of the schools and churches in the city were wrecked. The principal shopping areas were reduced to a low mass of rubble. Almost half the population of 220,000 left town, either for long stays or for the dark hours when the bombers came most frequently. Lady Astor danced with the Plymothians on the Hoe to keep up morale. But pictorial accounts recently published give a fearful impression of devastation, like those of Dresden or Berlin.

But I can remember that there was never a feeling of despair. And afterwards plans were quickly in hand for rebuilding Plymouth; as at Coventry, the destruction of the old narrow streets allowed for the creation of a modern city.

I think the new Plymouth is reasonably successful; from the utilitarian point of view the four parallel central streets offer easy access to shops, and Royal Parade, the main boulevard, is spacious and airy. Entering the city from the Tavistock, Exeter or Kingsbridge roads leads traffic to the roundabout in whose centre is the shell of bombed Charles Church, built in the seventeenth century and dedicated to King Charles the Martyr, a permanently touching memorial of the blitz.

Beyond it on the left is a group of buildings some of which survived the bombing or have been restored. St Andrew's Church is fifteenth-century and large, its Victorian and post-World War Two work good, with some windows by John Piper. Further along Royal Parade are lawns, the rebuilt Guildhall and the modern Civic Centre. Behind these are more churches of several denominations. Further on again are grouped cinemas, the television centre and the theatres.

Behind St Andrew's Church is medieval Prysten House, open to the public. I find my pleasure in visiting the ancient houses in Plymouth increased by the marvel of their having survived the bombing. The custodian of the Merchant's House, off Notte Street, told me that none of its great sturdy timbers were shaken out of true although buildings all around it were shattered, and no cracks appeared anywhere in the house. It is now a museum of local history, light and spacious, its three storeys served by a fine newel staircase. The granite-framed fireplaces were decorated with sgraffiti in the same manner as at Manor Farm, Strete.*

Further east along Notte Street, Southside Street is on the right. It traverses the Barbican, the oldest area of Plymouth still in existence. The word signifies the outer defence works of a fortified city, and the first Plymouth castle was sited near here. It is due to the Barbican Association that so much of the Elizabethan town remains today. New Street, parallel with and south of Southside Street, received the most intensive restoration. It is a narrow Elizabethan street, the upper storeys of some of the houses project over the street. They were restored and turned into flats and offices, and premises for shops and craftsmen. The back yards of Nos 34–40 were made into an Elizabethan garden to commemorate the 350th anniversary of the sailing of the *Mayflower* – a plaque on the West Pier wall, reached from the bottom end of New Street, marks this as well.

No. 32 New Street is one of the houses built for merchants and sea-captains, small but comfortable; its front living-room has mullion windows the width of the house-front and a panelled inner wall adjoining the passage through the house to the garden. There are three floors, the two upper ones reached by a newel stair, and a

* See p. 158.

cellar for mariner's goods, including perhaps some contraband! The custodian here tells how a maze of tunnels existed under the old streets, many of them uncovered by the bombing. These led to caves under the limestone cliffs, where stealthy boats brought the goods in under the noses of the excisemen.

Later, solid warehouses were put up in New Street to store prize goods during the Napoleonic Wars. By the end of 1971 the Association had rescued and restored over twenty properties in the Barbican area. It is now a tourist attraction with a crowded but pleasant miscellany of activities and amenities: shops offering clothes, chandlers, souvenirs and crafts. The elegant hall of the fish market lies east of the Mayflower Pier and adds a suitable real fishy tang, although the fishermen are fighting a desperate battle for survival. Island House, near the Mayflower Pier, and late sixteenth-century, is reputed to have been where the Pilgrim Fathers lodged.

At the north end of Southside Street is Coates Distillery, housed in a fourteenth-century Dominican priory. In its east end is a superb hall with a timbered arch-braced ceiling the shape of an upturned boat.

West of the Mayflower Pier the road leads uphill to the Hoe and Drake's statue. His stocky figure stands braced against the westerlies, calipers in his right hand touching the globe he circumnavigated, long sword at his side. The clawed feet of the globe-stand rest on bowls. The famous story of the game of bowls is most probably true; it was not purely gallant bravado that caused Drake to finish it, however, for he knew that even though the Armada was sweeping up-channel the English ships could not get out of Plymouth before wind and tide changed.

The Hoe is still the great central point of Plymouth. Its green sweep has accommodated gatherings through the centuries for games, meetings, executions, dancing and most recently peace rallies. As well as Drake's statue there is a large naval memorial to commemorate the sailors who died in the wars of this century, the Armada memorial of 1890, and Smeaton's lighthouse tower, brought from the reef fourteen miles out in the Channel when the present, fourth Eddystone lighthouse was erected in 1882. The first wooden one was destroyed in a storm in 1703, the second burned down in 1755. This year the light has been converted to automatic mechanism so that the lighthouse need no longer be manned. On clear days it is visible, with the stump of the old house beside it.

A block to the north of the Hoe, in Noote Street, William Cookworthy, the discoverer of china clay in England, held court to Dr Johnson, Captain Cook, Smeaton and many more. Nearby in Looe Street is Plymouth Arts Centre, opened as long ago as 1947 on the instigation of the Astors. Until recently the arts in Plymouth have played a small part in the life of the naval town. It is interesting now to see a flowering of artistic activity in the turbulent climate of the 1980s.

The entertainments provided for the maritime elements of the population traditionally consisted of bars, brothels and music-hall type theatre, although serious theatre did exist in Plymouth early in the eighteenth century as a result of the social life engendered by great families like the Edgcumbes at Mount Edgcumbe House and the Parkers at Saltram. In the present century came the cinemas and the decline of the theatres; in turn cinemas became bingo halls or were split into small auditoria. But the 1980s is seeing a resurrection of theatre. One of the largest theatres of the half-dozen or so operating in the late nineteenth century, the Palace Theatre of Varieties, opened in Union Street in 1898, with a décor of crimson plush and gilt art nouveau. After various closures and vicissitudes it reopened in 1978, staffed by a group of energetic local enthusiasts who repainted the interior in cream, green and gold. The exterior decoration has survived in its original form: at each end of the building, very high, are two simulated lighthouse towers, and tiled murals depict the Armada.

Enormous enterprise has been shown at Derry's Cross in the creation of Plymouth's new Theatre Royal, opened in 1982. Derry's clock is a small free-standing ornamental clock tower built by Plymouth Corporation in 1863 with financial aid from the then mayor, William Derry. The new theatre and other buildings dwarf the clock tower, beloved of Plymothians as one of the few buildings in this area to survive the blitz. The new theatre is a massive block with two stages and numerous amenities. An exhibition in one of its galleries of fine old prints of Plymouth and its surroundings seems to acknowledge that even this huge feat of modern cultural architecture cannot alter Plymouth's essentially maritime nature.

There are several important houses in the vicinity of Plymouth. I have mentioned Edgcumbe, and Drake's Buckland Abbey. Saltram

House lies on a rise on the east bank of the tidal Plym, where salt was probably panned by the Saxons. It is the former home of the Parker family, who took the title of Lords of Boringdon, their original home further east, and then Earls of Morley. The Tudor and Stuart buildings were enlarged into the present mid-eighteenth-century mansion, and John Foulston, nineteenth-century architect of many great Plymouth public and domestic buildings, created the library and entrance porch. Although I prefer smaller houses, I find Saltram a welcoming place. The furnishings are beautifully maintained and the house kept as if the family were just about to return, down to the smallest detail such as clean towels put out ready for use. Furniture, plate, carpets, silver are all magnificent. There is a fine collection of paintings. As well as a number of Joshua Reynolds' works, I especially like those by Angelica Kauffmann, one of the few women Royal Academicians of the eighteenth century; her strong, vital portraits are finely executed and coloured and her self-portrait is an autobiography.

Portraits are engaging, presenting a human being captured, whose eyes and personality can be gazed at for as long as desired without embarrassment to their owner; but holding their own counsel, withholding their confidence, the image only of the reality, after all. So it is with landscape and seascape painting, with photographs. You cannot reproduce the living person, the living world. Descriptive writing about them by one who sees with love may convey a little more of their elusive beauty and persona, their changing unchangeableness. For although we may cover the ground with buildings and hard roadways and pollute the rivers and seas, we shall be hard put to it to alter the contours of the high moor and the whaleback lowland hills, the winding courses of the rivers' lengths, the colours of the rocks, the stern battlements of the cliffs, and above all the sequence of the seasons. These are what matter most in South Devon.

Acknowledgements

I met and talked with so many people while preparing this celebration of South Devon. Those who particularly helped me include:

Sir Richard Acland; R. E. Andrews.

Dr Roger Beck; Povl, Christopher, Carrie and Crispin Born; W. Bowden-Smith.

Margaret Callaway; Mrs Henry Caunter; Lady Clifford; Terry Cook; Kay Coutin.

The Revd R. Denyer; Devon Centre for Further Education.

Len Fairweather; Nigel and Susan Fitzhughes.

Colin and Kate Gill; Tom Griffiths.

Dorothy Holman; W. G. Hoskins; Pop Hingston.

Robin Johnston.

Peter Kettleborough; Ursula Khan; Mark Kidel; Nan Kelly.

The librarians and archivists of the Bodleian Library, Oxford; Exeter Cathedral Library; Exeter City Library and West Country Studies Library; Ivybridge, Kingsbridge and Salcombe Libraries; Plymouth Record Office; Molly Lucas.

Christian Michell; Will and Molly Moore; Cyril Mulligan; David Murch; the staffs of the Castle Museum, Norwich; the Cookworthy Museum, Kingsbridge; the Devon Folk Life Register, Exeter City & County Museums Service; Salcombe Maritime Museum.

Dom Charles Norris; B. R. Northmoor.

Peter and Marianne Odling-Smee.

John Perkins; Mary Petter; Robert Pim; Vincent Piper; Mr and Mrs E. H. G. Pratt; Patricia Pratt.

Sam Richards; Stella Rogers.

Lawrence Sail; Geoffrey Savery; Dr J. B. Scrivenor; Mr and Mrs Silvester; Hubert Snowdon; South Brent WI; Jim and Alec Stone.

Kathy Tanner; Jonquil Tew; Harris Thorning; John Tucker.

Watts Blake Bearne & Co. Ltd; Mr and Mrs J. Weolbeoffe-Wilson; Peter White, DNP.

Jack Yeoman; Lord & Lady Young.

Select Bibliography

BARING-GOULD, SABINE. *Devon*, 1907; *Devonshire Characters and Strange Events*, 1908.

BRITISH REGIONAL GEOLOGY. *South West England*, HMSO, 1975.

CROSSING, WILLIAM. *Amid Devonia's Alps*, 1888; *A Hundred Years on Dartmoor*, 1901; *Dartmoor Worker*, c. 1903; *Dartmoor*, 1909.

CHOPE, R. P. (Ed.) *Early Tours in Devon and Cornwall*, 1918.

DEVON COUNTY COUNCIL PUBLICATIONS. *Doorway to Devon*, 1979; *Devon's Traditional Buildings*, 1979.

DIXON, SOPHIE. *A Journey of Eighteen Days on Dartmoor*, 1830.

DRAYTON, MICHAEL. *Polyolbion*, 1622.

EKWALL, E. *Oxford Dictionary of Place Names*, 1981.

FAIRWEATHER, JAMES. *Salcombe and Neighbourhood*, 1912.

FOX, S. P. *Kingsbridge Estuary with Rambles in the Neighbourhood*, 1864 (facsimile reproduction 1982).

GILL, CRISPIN. *Plymouth*, 1966/1981.

HAWKINS, ABRAHAM. *Kingsbridge and Salcombe, with the Intermediate Estuary, Historically and Topographically Depicted*, 1819.

HOSKINS, W. G. *Devon*, 1956; *Two Thousand Years in Exeter*, 1960.

HOPE and LLOYD, *Exeter Cathedral*, 1973.

LE MESSURIER, BRIAN. *South Devon Coast Path*, 1980.

LELAND, JOHN. *Itinerary in England and Wales*, c. 1535–43.

LUSCOMBE, ELLEN. *Myrtles and Aloes*, 1851.

MILLES, JEREMIAH. *Questionnaires*, c. 1755.

PAGE, J. L. W. *The Rivers of Devon*, 1893.

PERKINS, J. W. *Geology Explained in South and East Devon*, 1971; *Geology explained in Dartmoor and the Tamar Valley*, 1971.

PEVSNER, NIKOLAUS. *The Buildings of South Devon*, 1952.

The Place-Names of Devon. Cambridge, two volumes, 1931–32.

PRINCE, JOHN. *The Worthies of Devon*, 1701.

RISDON, TRISTRAM. *The Chorographical Description or Survey of the County of Devon*, 1630.

RUSSELL, PERCY. *Dartmouth*, 1950; *The Good Town of Totnes*, 1964.

SMITH, VIAN. *Portrait of Dartmoor*, 1966.

Victoria County History of Devon.

WESTCOTE, THOMAS. *A View of Devonshire in 1630*.

WESTCOTT, H. D. *The Devon South Coast Path*, 1982.

WILLY, MARGARET. *The South Hams*, 1955.

YOUNG, MICHAEL. *The Elmhirsts of Dartington*, 1982.

INDEX